24

™

THE OFFICIAL CTU
OPERATIONS MANUAL

BY

DENISE KIERNAN AND
JOSEPH D'AGNESE

QUIRK BOOKS
PHILADELPHIA

The authors would like to thank Virginia King, Rimma Aranovich, Mariana Galvez, and everyone on the *24* production team for their cooperation in producing this book.

24™ is produced in association with Real Time Productions.

Based on a series created by Joel Surnow & Robert Cochran

Library of Congress Cataloging in Publication Number: 2007932148

ISBN: 978-1-59474-197-5

Printed in China
Typeset in Eurostile, LCD, Russell Square, and Trade Gothic

Designed by Doogie Horner
Production management by Chris Veneziale

Photos on pages 59, 67, 69, 81, and 180 courtesy iStockphoto
Photo on page 184 courtesy Getty Images
Photo on page 68 courtesy NASA
Illustrations on pages 55, 56, 60, 61, and 112 by Paul Webb

Distributed in North America by Chronicle Books
680 Second Street
San Francisco, CA 94107

10 9 8 7 6 5 4 3 2 1

Quirk Books
215 Church Street
Philadelphia, PA 19106
www.quirkbooks.com

IN MEMORIAM

There are far too many brave and heroic CTU agents who have given their lives either in the line of duty or as a result of their commitment to their job. This manual is dedicated to all of those noble individuals, especially the following:

RICHARD WALSH

GEORGE MASON

GAEL ORTEGA

RYAN CHAPPELLE

MICHELLE DESSLER

EDGAR STILES

LYNN MCGILL

TONY ALMEIDA

CURTIS MANNING

MILO PRESSMAN

WELCOME TO THE COUNTER TERRORIST UNIT 10

by Jack Bauer

F INTERROGATION

G DISASTER MANAGEMENT

APPENDIX

039
038
037
036
035
034
033
032
031
030
029
028
027
026
025
024
023
022
021
020
019
018
017
016
015
014
013
012
011

WELCOME TO THE COUNTER TERRORIST UNIT

What makes a good CTU agent? That depends. Members of the Los Angeles CTU hail from a wide variety of backgrounds with as many different experiences. These differences give us our strength and our edge. And what bridges these differences, what brings us together under one roof, is our commitment to, love of, and respect for the way of life guaranteed to us by the Constitution of the United States of America.

Another thing we have in common is that we are all expendable.

I repeat: We are *all* expendable.

Being a CTU agent is about not only giving your best every day under every imaginable circumstance, but also doing your best while knowing full well that you may never get any recognition for your contributions. Indeed, some of us may give our lives, and many before you already have. Ego cannot be your motivation, nor can advancement. Your personal life, should you attempt to have one—and I strongly advise that you do not—will suffer. You will come to trust yourself alone, and when that trust falters, you too will falter.

The regulations put forth in this manual are not a set of suggestions. They are to be followed unless circumstance dictates otherwise. That said, all situations are different, and you should let your good judgment be your guide. The last thing I want to convey to any agent of CTU is this message: "Do as I say, not as I do." I have worked in a variety of capacities for CTU, and I am the first to acknowledge that I have not always followed the rules. But I was always willing, without a doubt, to accept the consequences that resulted from the choices I made. If you take it upon yourself to disregard CTU regulations and chain of command, be sure that you are willing to do the same.

Good luck. This nation, its citizens, and its president are counting on you.

JACK BAUER

Former Special Agent in Charge
and Director of Field Operations
CTU Los Angeles Domestic Unit

040
039
038
037
036
035
034
033
032
031
030
029
028
027
026
025
024
023
022
021
020
019
018
017
016
015
014
013
012

11

A	WORKING AT CTU

IN THIS SECTION, YOU WILL FIND INFORMATION ON THE BACK-
GROUND AND HISTORY OF CTU, PLUS A LIST OF YOUR NEW
RESPONSIBILITIES AND GENERAL GUIDELINES FOR OFFICE DRESS
AND COMPORTMENT. FAMILIARIZE YOURSELF WITH THIS MATERIAL
AS SOON AS POSSIBLE. YOU CANNOT FUNCTION WELL OUT THERE
UNLESS YOU KNOW WHAT IS EXPECTED OF YOU IN HERE.

040
039
038
037
036
035
034
033
032
031
030
029
028
027
026
025
024
023
022
021
020
019
018
017
016
015
014

AGENCY BACKGROUND

CTU grew out of Homeland Security's Counter Terrorism office when officials determined that the country would be better served by a separate agency operating independently and focusing solely on researching, identifying, tracking, and stopping terrorists and terrorist activities. CTU maintains active liaisons with a variety of agencies, most notably Homeland Security, the CIA, the Department of Defense, and the National Security Agency (NSA). CTU has, in the past, been at risk of being dismantled. On Day 5 of CTU history (reviewed on pages 44–45) during a terrorist attack involving Sentox nerve gas, a unit-wide backslash protocol was initiated and Homeland Security absorbed CTU, replacing many staff members and taking control of all active protocols. However, the absorption was only temporary.

If you are a field agent, you report to both the director of field operations and the assistant director. Analysts report to the Internet protocol manager and/or the senior analyst. The head of field ops and the senior analyst, in turn, report to the deputy director. The Special Agent in Charge (SAC) oversees all field and intelligence activities at CTU Los Angeles and reports directly to CTU Division Headquarters, which oversees all southern California operations. Division reports to our District Headquarters, which oversees all West Coast operations. All these offices are located in Los Angeles.

In the event that you have a complaint or concern regarding CTU operations, please proceed up the chain of command whenever possible. Do not go "over the head" of one of your immediate supervisors unless the information you have is justifiably sensitive.

044
043
042
041
040
039
038
037
036
035
034
033
032
031
030
029
028
027
026
025
024
023
022
021
020
019
018
017
016

045
044
043
042
041
040
039
038
037
036
035
034
033
032
031
030
029
028
027
026
025
024
023
022
021
020
019
018
017

THE SITUATION ROOM AT
CTU LOS ANGELES.

FIELD AGENTS VS. INTELLIGENCE AGENTS

The two main classes of agents at CTU Los Angeles are field agents and intelligence agents. The relationship between these two groups is the cornerstone of CTU's effectiveness in fighting and preventing terrorism. The coordination of their responsibilities and activities is overseen and managed by the SAC. There is to be no condescension from either group toward the other regarding whose role is more important. Neither can function effectively without the other. Although the agents' backgrounds and training may vary greatly, and personality differences may come into play, there is no room for attitude in this agency. When you come to work, leave your ego and personal prejudices at the door.

CLEARANCE LEVELS

CTU has established clearance levels from 1 through 6, with 1 being the lowest. Your level will be initially determined by the CTU SAC and will be subject to review every three months during your overall performance evaluations. During these evaluations, your immediate supervisor will consult with the SAC to determine whether or not the office will benefit from raising your clearance level. Clearance levels may also be raised temporarily during times of crisis or as your supervisor or SAC deems necessary. Do not take offense when your clearance is returned to its original level. This change is not a reflection on your performance.

Important: Keep your clearance level to yourself. This is not a playground, and your clearance level should not be a matter of bragging rights.

CTU STAFF INCLUDES INTELLIGENCE AGENTS (SUCH AS CHLOE O'BRIAN, ABOVE) AND FIELD AGENTS (LIKE THE LATE CURTIS MANNING, BELOW).

047
046
045
044
043
042
041
040
039
038
037
036
035
034
033
032
031
030
029
028
027
026
025
024
023
022
021
020
019

A2 OFFICES AND FACILITIES

CTU FLOOR PLAN AND EVACUATION PROCEDURES

A floor plan is posted on all floors, in all stairwells, and in all elevators. Familiarize yourself with it and note the exit nearest your workstation. Each department has a designated fire marshal who will brief you during your orientation about your department's off-site meeting point. Evacuation drills are conducted on a monthly basis and without notice. In the case of a Code 6 evacuation, save your work and then move calmly and quickly to the exits. Meet your department fire marshal at your designated area and wait for further instructions.

SAFE ZONES

As a precaution against a chemical or biological attack on CTU offices, safe zones are designated on the first and second floors and are equipped with bioseals. Ask your department fire marshal to identify the safe zone nearest your workstation.

ABOUT OUR HEALTH CLINIC

Our clinic is now fully equipped to handle most medical emergencies and to perform surgeries. Medical personnel are at your disposal twenty-four hours a day. We would like to remind you, however, that the clinic's first and foremost priority is to provide medical services in support of CTU's overall mission and active protocols. Be aware that in the event your treatment is deemed secondary to the treatment of a hostile possessing information vital to national security, your treatment will be suspended until the hostile has been stabilized. If you do not agree with this policy, you should reexamine your commitment to CTU's mission and objectives.

Mental health counseling, including stress management, is available through an off-site counselor. All counselors have been prescreened and approved by CTU. We respect the doctor-patient privilege, but you are nevertheless restricted from discussing classified information and details of current and past protocols.

ADDITIONAL FACILITIES

- **CTU Walsh Memorial Library:** Our library houses one of the most extensive collections of military and intelligence journals and academic papers on the West Coast. It is at your disposal and staffed by some of the country's most experienced reference librarians. The library also hosts weekly lectures and guest speakers. Consult the bulletin board for a schedule.

048
047
046
044
043
042
041
040
039
038
037
036
035
034
033
032
031
030
029
028
027
026
025
024
023
022
021
020
19

049
048
047
046
045
044
043
042
041
040
039
038
037
036
035
034
033

THIS CONFERENCE ROOM IS ONE OF
SEVERAL DESIGNATED SAFE ZONES
LOCATED IN THE BUILDING.

032
031
030
029
028
027
026
025
024
023
022
021

- **Child Care:** Due to the nature of our work, our stringent security measures, and the safety risk that is posed to any and all CTU employees, child care is not provided on-site. This policy has been debated by various members of CTU, and prior child-care crises have prompted us to review our facilities. At times, small children have been brought into the office without prior consent. This is strictly forbidden. For child-care providers in the area that have been certified by CTU, please see the list posted in the break room on the main floor.

- **Parking:** All parking is on-site and free of charge. Always park in your assigned space. *Never* let friends or family members "borrow" your space or parking pass, as that is in violation of our security policy.

- **Fitness center, showers, and locker room:** The fitness center features state-of-the-art equipment for physical conditioning and strength training, including weight equipment, treadmills, and stationary bicycles. Visit the center for hours and a schedule of classes. The locker room and showers are available twenty-four hours a day and should be kept as neat and tidy as possible. If you are operating undercover and anticipate working on-site at CTU, be sure to store appropriate office attire in your locker.

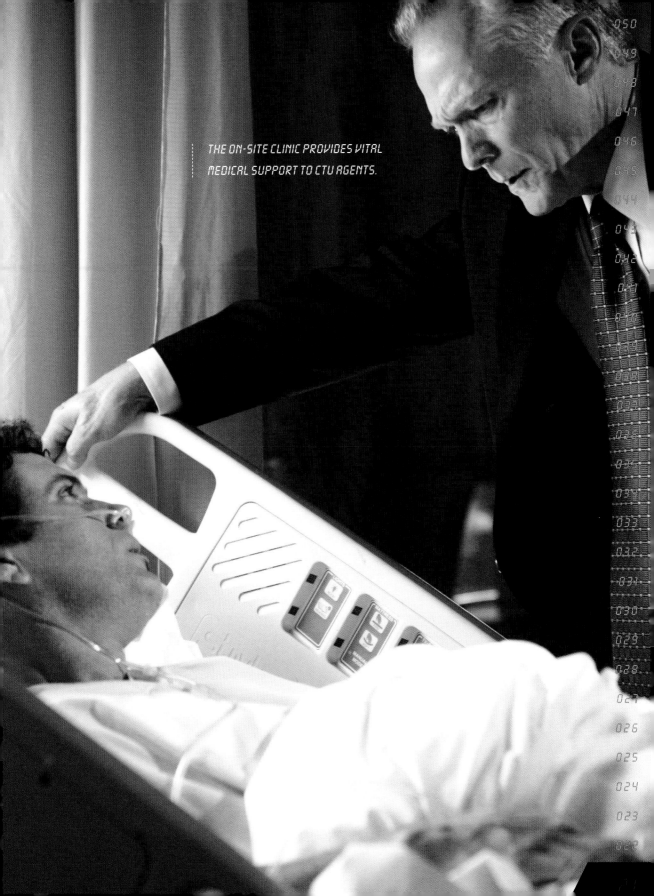

THE ON-SITE CLINIC PROVIDES VITAL
MEDICAL SUPPORT TO CTU AGENTS.

050
049
048
047
046
045
044
043
042
041
040
039
038
037
036
035
034
033
032
031
030
029
028
027
026
025
024
023
022

051
050
049
048
047
046
045
044
043
042
041
040
039
038
037
036
035
034
033
032
031
030
029
028
027
026
025
024
023

- **Commissary:** The commissary is open daily and accepts cash, credit cards, or CTU dining cards. No guests are permitted in the commissary. Food and beverages are highly sensitive, and an attack on these items could quickly cripple our agency. With that in mind, chemical analysts from our forensic lab are always available to test any foods or beverages prior to consumption if it is believed that our supply has been compromised.
  - **Firing ranges:** There are two primary ranges: One is on-site, located on sub-level 2. The other is a long-range shooting facility located off-site. To schedule time in the firing range, please see the chief armorer.

REGULATIONS AND CODES OF CONDUCT

Whether working at the CTU offices, operating in the field, or merely acting in public as a private citizen, you are always expected to conduct yourself in a manner that reflects well on the Counter Terrorist Unit and the United States of America. Your status as a federal agent of this country is not something that you put on like a uniform. It is an honor that you carry with you with pride, no matter where you are, who you are with, and what you are doing.

CTU POLICY ON FRATERNIZATION

A career as a CTU agent is a serious commitment, and leaving your job at the office is not an easy task. We acknowledge that spending so much time at work and having a job that becomes a part of virtually every aspect of your life can make it difficult to know where your professional life ends and your personal life begins. For this reason, it is also not unusual for agents to develop relationships that exceed those parameters defined by their jobs. Although CTU understands that these relationships are unplanned and may develop naturally, CTU is not your typical agency. It is our stated policy to strongly discourage romantic relationships among our agents.

In the past, agency officials have looked the other way when these romances have been made public. A much stricter stance is now being taken for the safety and security of the agency and our country. The importance of this new stance is borne out by past interoffice romances that have compromised not only missions but lives as well.

052
051
050
049
048
047
046
045
044
043
042
041
040
039
038
037
036
035
034
033
032
031
030
029
028
027
026
025
024
23

CTU STRONGLY DISCOURAGES ROMANTIC RELATIONSHIPS BETWEEN AGENTS.

MIND YOUR CONVERSATIONS.

Never discuss work with anyone who does not have the proper clearance, no matter what kind of relationship you have with them. A security breach is a security breach. Emotional bonds do not supersede established clearance levels.

STAY OBJECTIVE.

This advice is perhaps the most difficult for any individual in a romantic relationship to follow, but should you decide to disregard CTU policy on interoffice romance, you must do your best to take it to heart. The cliché "love is blind" is dangerously accurate. Two of our most highly trained and decorated agents were romantically involved with an agent who turned out to be a traitor. On Day 6, Milo Pressman's feelings for Nadia Yassir prompted him to come forward as acting CTU director in her stead while CTU was besieged by Chinese mercenaries acting under the direction of Cheng Zhi. This romantically charged act of bravery cost him his life.

053
052
051
050
049
048
047
046
045
044
043
042
041
040
039
038
037
036
035
034
033
032
031
030
029
028
027
026
025
24

ACTING DIRECTOR LYNN MCGILL
WAS REMOVED FROM HIS POST
UNDER THE TERMS AND
CONDITIONS OF SECTION 1.12.

054
053
052
051
050
049
048
047
046
045
044
043
042
041
040
039
038
037
036
035
034
033
032
031
030
029
028
027
026

NEVER LOSE SIGHT OF YOUR MISSION.

Stay focused. Do not let your opinions or feelings interfere with decision making. If you think that your relationship might be affecting your ability to do your job—it is.

A WORD ABOUT FAMILIES.

CTU understands the importance of family. However, always be aware that your family can become a liability if your enemies know who and where your loved ones are. Many agents have lost family members because of their work with CTU, and others have experienced the threat of such a loss. Family loyalty and mission priorities also conflict at times. As demonstrated in the CTU case history for Day 3, the marriage between Agent Almeida and Agent Dessler interfered with Almeida's ability to execute his post as SAC of CTU. It not only cost Almeida his job but also sent him to jail. As Brad Hammond from Division explained to a dismayed Agent Dessler: "Tony has a sworn duty to protect the people of this country. Putting your life first was treasonous. And he's going to prison for it. So will you."

IDENTIFYING AN UNSTABLE SUPERIOR

CTU's agency charter permits the removal of the highest-ranking official at CTU if he or she is deemed mentally unfit for duty. In this case, the incapacity clause of Section 1.12 must be invoked by the next-to-highest-ranking officer. The person in question may be detained and removed from the floor, but this action must be reviewed as soon as possible by district personnel. To be found just, the action must meet the following requirements or be supported by the following evidence:

- Two or more witnesses—other than the second-highest-ranking official—attest that, prior to his or her removal, the highest-ranking official had demonstrated erratic behavior, poor judgment, or questionable conduct that would jeopardize CTU personnel or the active protocol. CTU review boards have ruled that "erratic behavior, poor judgment, and jeopardy-inducing conduct" is behavior such as:
  - Abusive, profane, and inciting language or physical actions directed at CTU personnel.
  - Stubborn insistence on the following of orders that seem to be inconsistent, unproductive, and unwarranted in light of the facts of the active protocol.
  - Mentally unstable behavior consistent with a psychological impairment.
  - Disturbing behavior or directives that appear to be conducted for the sole purpose of self-aggrandizement.
- Logs, databases, or digitally encoded or hard-copy documentation that supports the staff's assessment that the official behaved in a manner inconsistent with that of a sound and prudent superior confronted with similar information, facts, or events.

055
054
053
052
051
050
049
048
047
046
045
044
043
042
041
040

039
038
037
036
035
034
033
032
031
030
029
028
027

THOUGH OFFICIALLY RELIEVED OF DUTY, MCGILL SAVED THE LIVES OF EVERYONE AT CTU.

- The superior in question was warned by his second-in-command to reconsider the questionable actions, commands, or directives but refused to do so.

- Clear, compelling evidence that the second-in-command did not simply disagree with a superior but found that person's behavior to be truly detrimental to the CTU protocol, mission, or staff and had no other adequate remedy except the enactment of Section 1.12.

IMPORTANT

Employees are reminded that any superior who is relieved of duty under Section 1.12 should still be treated with courtesy, even while being detained. District draws a sharp distinction between superiors removed under the incapacity clause and those removed under suspicion of being a mole or traitor. Do not confuse the two. See the next section for more details.

MANY CTU EMPLOYEES SUSPECTED AGENT GAEL ORTEGA OF BEING A MOLE. HE WAS LATER REVEALED TO BE WORKING ON A TOP-SECRET UNDERCOVER STING OPERATION.

056
055
054
053
052
051
050
049
048
047
046
045
044
043
042
041
040
039
038
037
036
035
034
033
032
031
030
029
028

IDENTIFYING MOLES AND TRAITORS

Moles are called that for a reason: They're dirty and shifty and excel at operating below the surface. However, the following behavioral characteristics and habits may help you identify a potential mole in your midst:

- He or she is overly ambitious.
- He or she seeks favor with superiors and seems more concerned with promotion than accomplishing the mission objective.
- He or she is overly interested in the work of others. When someone is more interested in what his or her neighbor is working on than in the assigned task, notice should be taken. No one at CTU should have idle time to look over another's shoulder.

055
054
053
052
051
050
049
048
047
046
045
044
043
042
041
040
038
037
036
033
032
031
030
029

JAMEY FARRELL

NINA MY

MARIANNE TAYLOR

WALT CUMMIN

058
057
056
055
054
053
052
051
050
049
048
047
046
045
044
043
042
041
040
039
038
037
036
035
034
033
032
031
030

- He or she takes frequent bathroom breaks. One of the most private and loosely monitored areas of CTU is the bathroom, and it often serves as a private setting where moles can conduct their business away from prying eyes and ears. Also, bathroom breaks are often used as an excuse to cover attempts to gain access to areas of CTU headquarters that would otherwise be off limits or to sabotage infrastructure.

- He or she requests clearance and access beyond his or her security level. At CTU, we are all team players. Everyone at every clearance level has an important job to do. Those—especially without adequate experience—who repeatedly seek ways to gain greater access should be carefully monitored.

- Moles are often troublemakers. They will seek to exploit relationship conflicts between agents and even blackmail others for information or clearance privileges.

HOW TO FLUSH OUT A MOLE

Moles are most often trafficking in information, our most valuable commodity. Once they have the intel, they must communicate it quickly and efficiently to their employers or co-conspirators. If a security breach is suspected and all evidence points to the existence of a mole, an efficient way to flush out the mole is to dangle the carrot of information as bait and then watch who takes it. Here's one approach:

Begin by devising false information relating to an active, high-priority protocol that is already in progress. Only a few key individuals can know about the operation. Call a meeting. Be dramatic. Make sure everyone in attendance firmly believes that the information being shared is highly classified and applies directly to an active protocol of the highest priority. Then monitor all communications going into and out of the building immediately following the dissemination of the "classified" information. The mole will want to find a way to transmit the information as quickly as possible. Monitoring and recording all COM will reveal not only the mole but possibly the mole's contact as well.

I M P O R T A N T

It is possible for a seasoned mole with excellent technical training to filter his or her communications or even route them through another agent's system. If the suspected mole doesn't feel "right" to you, try to gauge whether you should follow your gut and continue your mole hunt. Obviously, if important information continues to find its way into the wrong hands, you'll know for sure that you have the wrong person. Beware of setups. CTU employees have been falsely accused and unnecessarily tortured as a result of carefully orchestrated framing.

059
058
057
056
055
054
053
052
051
050
049
048
047
046
045
044
043
042
041
040
039
038
037
036
035
034
033
032
031

ADDITIONAL STRATEGIES

- **Keep a close eye on things.** If necessary, the SAC may choose to impose a Section 2.3 redundancy to monitor the work of others. In this case, all the work of the selected individual(s) will be mirrored through the SAC's computer. This option should be employed only if absolutely necessary since its misuse can severely damage levels of trust and respect.

- **Do not act hastily.** Before you take action against the character and reputation of a colleague at CTU, be sure that you have all your facts straight. Always keep in mind that you may not possess all the information to make a proper and accurate assessment of the situation. As discussed in the CTU case history for Day 3 (pages 40–41), things are not always what they seem. Agent Gael Ortega, believed to be conspiring with the Salazar crime family, was, in fact, ultimately revealed to be working on a highly secretive undercover sting operation with Agent Jack Bauer and Agent Tony Almeida.

- **Initiating a lockdown.** In the event of a security breach or suspicion of a mole, a lockdown may be initiated by an agent of CTU. While under lockdown, *no one* is allowed to leave the premises. All computers will be frozen and communication into and out of the building will be disabled. A lockdown will remain in effect until representatives from Division arrive on-site and determine, to their satisfaction, that any security breach has been averted or contained and that the responsible parties have been identified.

SAFEGUARDING YOUR KEY CARD

All CTU employees are issued key cards upon signed acceptance of an employment offer. Your photo, name, signature, and select biometric data are digitally encoded, though these personalized cards will forever remain the property of CTU. You are expected to keep this key card on your person at all times, to present it when requested by your superiors or by CTU security, and to surrender it upon the conclusion of your employment at CTU. Key cards are intended for three purposes only:

1. To gain access to CTU facilities and specific work areas or rooms within those facilities.
2. To transport data between one CTU computer and another.
3. To share active protocols with others in your work group.

Please note that if you need to analyze media from an internal or external source—such as CDs, DVDs, flash drives, and the like—you must use your key card to unlock and activate any of the conventional drives on your computer. This measure is done for security purposes.

A STOLEN KEY CARD LED TO THE DEMISE OF ONE OF CTU'S TOP INTELLI- GENCE ANALYSTS, EDGAR STILES.

060
059
058
057
056
055
054
053
052
051
050
049
048
047
046
045
044
043
042
041
040
039
038
037
036
035
034
033
032
031

061
060
059
058
057
056
055
054
053
052
051
050
049
048
047
046
045
044
043
042
041
040
039
038
037
036
035
034
033

IMPORTANT

Your key card is your digital identity. Take all necessary precautions to safeguard your card while on and off CTU premises. Never display, discuss, or share your card with anyone who is not a CTU employee on active status. This precaution is for your own security and the security of your fellow employees. Stolen cards have resulted in the infiltration of our facility by enemies of this nation and resulted in the death of numerous staff members. (See case study, Day 5, on pages 44–45.) Report all lost and stolen cards immediately to your SAC or supervisor. Any employee who intentionally allows a key card to fall into the hands of non-CTU individuals is subject to disciplinary charges, arrest, and possible prison term.

EMPLOYEE DRESS CODE

Work at CTU can be stressful. Specific protocols may run for many hours, and we want you to be as comfortable as possible in your work wear. However, we are a federal agency, and a certain acceptable level of dress is required while on the premises, as expressed by the dress code explained below:

Sturdy, comfortable shoes must be worn at all times. During an attack or other emergency, you must be able to evacuate quickly. Open-toed shoes, sandals, and similar foot apparel is forbidden. Footwear that is garishly colored, emits bright lights, doubles as rollerskates, or the like may make you a target and is thus forbidden as well.

Clothing depicting insignias, logos, commercial brands, conspicuous artwork, political statements, and the like is strictly forbidden. You may display CTU logos or a lapel pin of the U.S. flag, but be aware that such accoutrements may not be appropriate during certain sensitive field operations and undercover missions.

The "casual" look—i.e., open-collared shirts—is acceptable for men and women. But please be aware that ties and jackets for men, and business suits for women, may be expected during certain high-level functions and meetings. No worn jeans, shorts, "low-riders," halter tops, tank tops, frayed or worn garments, or bare-shoulder blouses are ever permitted in work areas. If you wear a T-shirt, it must be clean, pressed, and accompanied by a jacket or blazer.

Employees using the agency fitness center are expected to wear clothing emblazoned with official CTU logos.

Female employees are not permitted to wear skirts that fall higher than two inches above the knee.

Flash drives, electronic headphones, MP3 players, and other consumer electronics—including your personal mobile phone, PDA, and pager—must be checked with the security desk upon arrival each morning. Non-CTU-issued laptop computers are not permitted at any time on or near the premises. Use of CTU-issued mobile phones, pagers, and PDAs are permitted. You may use these devices for personal calls, but keep the communications brief.

Only bona fide members of the U.S. armed services may wear U.S. military uniforms, camo, or other such garments on CTU premises. At no time will the wearing of foreign military gear, artifacts, curios, or memorabilia be permitted except by approved visiting foreign personnel with proper clearances. If you are dispatched to the field and require mission-appropriate clothing and gear, it will be provided by CTU. See section B for details (page 49).

Facial hair is permitted as long as it is neatly groomed. Please be aware that goatees, "soul patches," and outlandish mustache/beard combinations may be interpreted as "sinister" by members of the public and may cause you to be targeted in the event of public unrest. Use discretion.

EMPLOYEES MUST FOLLOW
CTU DRESS CODE WHILE ON-SITE.

KEEP HAIR NEATLY GROOMED

OPEN-COLLARED SHIRTS
ARE ACCEPTABLE

CARRY KEY CARD
AT ALL TIMES

BLUE JEANS ARE ACCEPTABLE

STURDY, COMFORTABLE
SHOES ARE MANDATORY

SELECTED CASE STUDIES:
THE SIX MOST IMPORTANT DAYS
IN CTU HISTORY

CTU'S HISTORY IS FULL OF EXAMPLES THAT DEMONSTRATE BOTH HOW TO DO THINGS AND HOW NOT TO DO THINGS. THE SIX CASE STUDIES PRESENTED HERE MAY BE SHORT, BUT THE INFORMATION THEY CONTAIN RELATES TO MANY OF OUR KEY REGULATIONS AND POLICIES. READ THESE CASE STUDIES CAREFULLY. THE DETAILS HEREIN FORM THE BASIS OF MANY OF THE TRAINING AND PROCEDURAL EXAMPLES THAT WE WILL REFER TO THROUGHOUT THIS MANUAL.

DAY 1

The events of Day 1 found CTU agents racing against time to prevent the assassination of Senator David Palmer by a well-coordinated team of international and domestic assassins. The events took place on the day of the California presidential primary. The CTU investigation was led by Agent Bauer, assisted by Agents Almeida and Myers. Complicating our investigation was the fact that both Agent Bauer's wife, Teri, and daughter Kim had been kidnapped on the very same day by a gang led by Ira Gaines. An American-trained mercenary, Gaines had been hired to kill Palmer and frame Bauer for the crime, using his family as leverage. But when Bauer disrupted the plot—saving Palmer, rescuing Teri and Kim Bauer, and killing Gaines—the true orchestrators of the day's events kicked into Plan B. They were Andre and

01:27:09

065
064
063
062
061
060
059
058
057
056
055
054
053
052
051
050
049
048
047
046
045
044
043
042
041
040
039
038

Alexis Drazen, sons of the Serbian genocidal maniac Victor Drazen, believed killed during Operation Nightfall, a U.S.-sponsored covert op led by none other than Bauer two years prior to Day 1. The Drazens were carrying out a vicious two-year-old vendetta against Bauer and Palmer, who had authorized the Nightfall mission. Unbeknownst to CTU and agencies with which we liaise, Drazen had in fact survived the attack and was incarcerated for two years in a secret U.S. government prison. Mercenaries hired by his sons managed to free him, but only for a short time. Agent Bauer infiltrated their organization, rescued his daughter yet again, and terminated the Drazens. At day's end, much to the horror of all at CTU, Agent Myers was revealed to have been working as a mole, feeding intel throughout the day to the Drazen organization. She was captured, but not before she killed Teri Bauer.

066
065
064
063
062
061
060
059
058
057
056
055
054
053
052
051
050
049

048
047
046
045
044
043
042
041
040
039

DAY 2

On this day, CTU was charged with locating and disposing of a nuclear warhead known to be in Los Angeles and set to detonate imminently. The bomb's handlers were believed to be a foreign organization known as Second Wave. To pick up the group's trail, Agent Bauer—summoned from inactive duty—went undercover, infiltrating a domestic anti-government group led by his former arrestee, Joseph Wald. (Wald had apparently received plans of our facility from traitor Nina Myers.) While undercover, Bauer watched in horror as his hostile cohorts successfully bombed CTU headquarters, killing at least thirty agents. This attack was intended to divert attention from Syed Ali's plot to detonate the bomb over the city from the helm of a Cessna aircraft. Following clues emanating from the financial dealings of the Warners, a prominent Los Angeles family, Agent Bauer extracted the location of the bomb from the captured Ali. When the bomb could not be defused, Bauer volunteered for the sacrificial mission—approved and coordinated with President David Palmer—to drop the bomb in the Mojave Desert. In the final

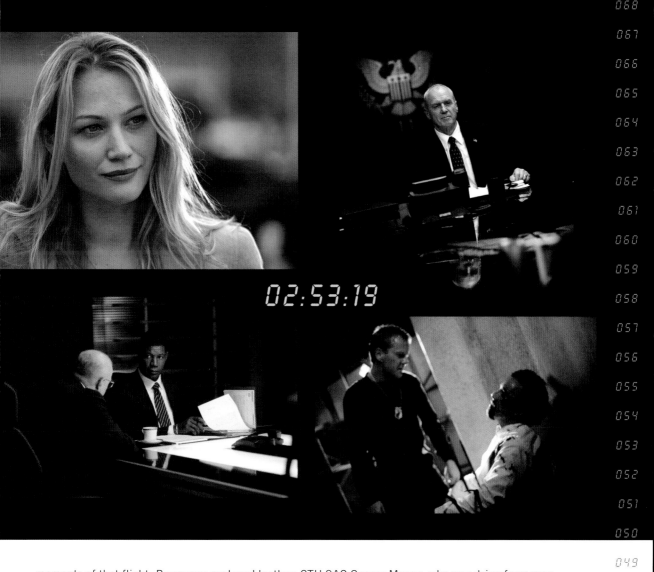

02:53:19

068
067
066
065
064
063
062
061
060
059
058
057
056
055
054
053
052
051
050
049
048
047
046
045
044
043
042
041
040
39

moments of that flight, Bauer was replaced by then-CTU SAC George Mason, who was dying from exposure to plutonium that he had suffered earlier that day. Making the ultimate sacrifice, Mason successfully crashed the plane into the desert floor. Even before the vast mushroom cloud bloomed in the sky, President Palmer was under pressure by administration officials to retaliate against three nations believed to have harbored the terrorists. The only evidence of their involvement was the so-called Cyprus recording. CTU raced to verify the recording's authenticity, but Palmer's reluctance to attack led his vice president and cabinet to invoke Section 4 of the Twenty-fifth Amendment, removing him from office because they believed him unfit to lead. The recording was ultimately revealed to be a forgery, the creation of a Euro-American oil cartel with holdings in the Caspian Sea. On this evidence, the president was reinstated, U.S. fighter planes were recalled at the last possible second, and war was averted. Soon after, however, Palmer was exposed to a dangerous biological weapon by a hired assassin known only as Mandy.

068
067
066
065
064
063
062
061
060
059
058
057
056
055
054
053
052
051

050
049
048
047
046
045
044
043
042
041

DAY 3

This day's events centered on the potential sale and release of the deadly Cordilla virus by terrorists with past ties to Agent Jack Bauer and CTU. When a dead body infected with the virus was deposited outside the National Health Services Building, CTU scrambled to find out who had control of the virus and whether more attacks were planned. CTU was contacted by the Salazar crime family, who demanded that their brother and leader, Ramon, be released from prison to prevent further attacks. The true danger was then believed to be the sale of mass quantities of this weaponized virus on the terrorist market. The Salazars were potential buyers who had been undercover with Salazar in the past and who, along with Director Tony Almeida and Agent Gael Ortega, had devised a long-term sting operation to put Bauer back into play with the Salazars and confiscate the virus. Bauer—still struggling with a heroin addiction acquired during his earlier operation—broke Salazar out of prison to reestablish his cover, but

070
069
068
067
066
065
064
063
062
061
060
059
058
057
056
055
054
053
052

03:10:05

051
050
049
048
047
046
045
044
043
042
041

attempts by CTU to recover the virus failed. It was soon discovered that the virus was in the hands of Stephen Saunders, a former MI6 agent who worked with Agent Bauer on Operation Nightfall and was left for dead. CTU could not prevent the release of the virus at the Chandler Plaza Hotel in Los Angeles, where Agent Michelle Dessler led the operation to contain guests and prevent an outbreak. At least 800 lives were lost. Dessler was taken hostage by Saunders, who used her as leverage to force her husband, Almeida, to thwart a siege by CTU on Saunders's offices. Saunders had successfully placed dispersal devices containing the virus in the hands of his terrorist operatives across the country, and it was not until the life of his own daughter was threatened that he began cooperating with CTU and revealed the locations of the remaining devices. Almeida's critical mistake—placing the life of his wife above the lives of all American citizens—cost him his job and sent him to prison.

071
070
069
068
067
066
065
064
063
062
061
060
059
058
057
056
055
054
053
052
051
050
049
048
047
046
045
044
043

DAY 4

On this day, CTU stopped terrorists who unleashed a series of coordinated events, culminating with the infamous attack on Air Force One and the launch of a U.S. nuclear missile on American soil. First, the organization, led by Habib Marwan, kidnapped Secretary of Defense James Heller and his senior policy analyst and daughter, Audrey Raines, to try the secretary for so-called crimes against humanity. Heller and Raines were rescued by Agent Bauer and U.S. Marines, but Internet traffic surrounding the "trial" had masked the fact that Marwan's group was using the Internet to tap into the mainframes of 104 U.S. nuclear power plants with an electronic tool called the Dobson Override. This device, developed by defense contractors McLennan-Forster to help manage multiple nuclear energy operations from a central location, had been stolen by Marwan, a former McLennan-Forster employee, and was used to initiate what could have been a devastating series of coast-to-coast meltdowns. CTU analysts stopped all but one reactor—on San Gabriel Island—from melting down, but the loss of life and damage from fall-

072
071
070
069
068
067
066
065
064
063
062
061
060
059
058
057
056
055
054

04:53:19

out were considerable. Terrorists then stole a stealth fighter and attacked Air Force One. With President John Keeler in critical condition, Vice President Charles Logan was immediately sworn in as president. From the plane's crash site, Marwan's men seized critical codes from the nuclear football and subsequently used them to launch a stolen U.S. missile at Los Angeles. Marwan proved to be a difficult target but eventually died during apprehension, and information from his PDA was used to pinpoint the missile's trajectory and safely shoot down the weapon. During the investigation, the Chinese consulate was apparently invaded, and a Chinese national with ties to Marwan was apprehended. The death of the Chinese consul from friendly fire angered the Chinese, who claimed the mission had been headed by Bauer. The U.S. government vehemently denied involvement, but the resulting fiasco prompted Agent Bauer to fake his own death and leave his old life behind. A shaken nation was left to heal under the leadership of President Logan.

053
052
051
050
049
048
047
046
045
044

43

WORKING AT CTU   A4

DAY 5

On the day of a historic accord between the United States and Russia, former president David Palmer was assassinated, and former CTU agents Michelle Dessler and Tony Almeida were attacked in a car bombing. Dessler was killed, and Almeida was left in critical condition. Evidence pointed to Agent Bauer, who was presumed dead. Bauer emerged from hiding to clear his name and became embroiled in a day-long chain of events that led to the top of the U.S. government. At first, the day's events were believed to have been orchestrated in part by President Logan's chief of staff, Walt Cummings, who confessed that he had engaged in a plot to plant a canister containing the dangerous nerve agent Sentox aboard a freighter bound for Asia and later manipulated events to support an increased U.S. military presence in that region. But somehow Cummings and his handlers were double-crossed, and the plot went seriously awry. Russian separatists used a tragic hostage situation at Ontario Airport to gain possession of the Sentox, which they used successfully in a pair of attacks—one on the Sunrise Hills Mall and, later, one on CTU premises. Regrettably, the latter killed 40 percent of CTU active staff.) At least two other major

05:36:42

074
073
072
071
070
069
068
067
066
065
064
063
062
061
060
059
058
057
056
055
054
053
052
051
050
049
048
047
046
45

attacks were thwarted during the day: one upon a motorcade carrying the Russian president, his wife, and the First Lady to the airport, and a second at a local hospital where the terrorists intended to release more Sentox. Agent Bauer tracked the gas's origins to a company called Omicron, which employed Christopher Henderson, his mentor and former CTU director of field operations. Henderson clearly knew more than he was revealing, but all efforts to extract intel from him using medical means failed. He killed Agent Almeida and escaped. Following the attack on CTU headquarters, Homeland Security assumed control of CTU. Shortly after, audio evidence surfaced that implicated Henderson and another man in the conspiracy to kill Palmer and to place the Sentox in the hands of the terrorists. Henderson was eventually tracked and killed by Agent Bauer, but the other man survived, using all the power at his disposal to sidetrack CTU and kill Bauer. But with the help of the First Lady, Charles Logan was also eventually unmasked for what he was: a traitor to the nation. Following conclusion of the case, Agent Bauer was abducted by the Chinese government and transported by boat to China.

075
074
073
072
071
070
069
068
067
066
065
064
063
062
061
060
059
058
057
056
055
054
053
052
051
050
049
048
047

DAY 6

On Day 6, newly elected president Wayne Palmer arranged for the release of Agent Bauer from the Chinese prison in which he had been held for the last two years. Bauer had been sent there in retaliation for his actions against the Chinese consulate on Day 4. After a series of suicide bombings in the United States that killed 900 Americans, the president agreed to swap Bauer for information leading to the arrest of Amri al-Hassad, the plan's alleged architect. Upon discovering that al-Hassad was trying to stop the bombings, Bauer escaped from his captor, Abu Fayed, who had orchestrated the swap to cover up a more nefarious plot: the detonation of five nuclear bombs enclosed in small suitcases. Regrettably, despite Bauer's and CTU's best efforts, one of the bombs was detonated in Valencia, California, killing about 12,000. The remaining suitcase nukes escaped in the hands of Fayed and his co-conspirator, former Soviet general Dmitri Gredenko, who sought to launch the bombs from aerial drones. Two of the central players in the day's events were none other than Phillip and Graem Bauer, Agent Bauer's estranged father and brother. The pair, who headed military contractor BXJ Technologies, had secretly manipulated former President Charles Logan during Day 5 to further their oil interests. During his investigation, Agent Bauer learned that his two family members had also been responsible for the deaths of President David Palmer and former CTU agents Michelle Dessler and Tony Almeida. Following CTU-led field interrogation, Graem was killed by his father, who escaped. Meanwhile, a gang

076
075
074
073
072
071
070
069
068
067
066
065
064
063
062

06:43:22

061
060
059
058
057
056
055
054
053
052
051
050
049
048

of radical patriots within the White House attempted to assassinate President Palmer but succeeded only in severely wounding him. Vice President Noah Daniels assumed temporary control of the nation's highest office. Subsequently, CTU managed to halt one launched drone, locate the remaining suitcase bombs, and kill Gredenko and Fayed. But the day did not end there. Agent's Bauer's former captor, Chinese operative Cheng Zhi, surfaced and announced that he was holding hostage Audrey Raines—daughter of former Secretary of Defense James Heller—in exchange for a Russian-built subcircuit board from one of the nukes. A deceptive swap, covertly endorsed by a recovering President Palmer, was rescinded by Vice President Daniels when the president lapsed back into a coma. International tension and the threat of war mounted when the Russian government learned that the Chinese had gained access to the chip through a bungled government attempt to stop Agent Bauer's mission. As Vice President Daniels engaged in sensitive talks with the Russians, CTU worked to regain the chip, which had been damaged in transit. Phillip Bauer agreed to repair it for Cheng in exchange for his grandson Josh, whom he apparently wished to take forcibly to China, where he had been granted asylum. Working with dismissed Agent Bill Buchanan, Agent Bauer raided the oil rig where Cheng and Phillip Bauer were to rendezvous, killed several of Cheng's men, captured Cheng, rescued his nephew, and left his wounded father to be bombed into oblivion in a U.S.-led military strike.

8	GEAR

THE COUNTER TERRORIST UNIT MAINTAINS A VAST ARRAY OF THE MOST UP-TO-DATE AND CUTTING-EDGE FIELD EQUIPMENT TO SUPPORT OUR AGENTS IN TACTICAL FIELD OPERATIONS. BOTH FIELD AND INTELLIGENCE AGENTS ARE EXPECTED TO FAMILIARIZE THEMSELVES WITH THE FUNCTIONING OF THIS EQUIPMENT. AS YOU DO SO, KEEP IN MIND THAT THIS VERY SAME EQUIPMENT MAY SOMEDAY BE USED AGAINST YOU. WELL-FUNDED TERRORIST ORGANIZATIONS OFTEN HAVE UNLIMITED BUDGETS AND HAVE THE SAME TACTICAL RESOURCES AS OUR AGENCY. FOR THIS REASON, ALWAYS REMEMBER: GEAR IS NO SUBSTITUTE FOR QUICK THINKING, EFFECTIVE DECISION-MAKING IN THE FIELD, AND PERSONAL RESOLVE.

079
078
077
076
075
074
073
072
071
070
069
068
067
066
065
064
063
062
061
060
059
058
057
056
055
054
053
052
051

B1 | FIELD AGENT SUPPLY CHECKLIST

CTU's chief armorer is responsible for outfitting vehicles and maintaining weapons and surveillance kits. Yet prior to deployment, individual agents should always double-check that they have the necessary gear.

CLOTHING

Body armor, including Kevlar vests and other flak jackets, is standard issue and should be worn whenever possible. CTU provides all grades of protection, from Type I to Type IV. Some agents prefer not to be encumbered by vests while in the field, but we cannot stress strongly enough the benefits of this added layer of protection.

CTU VEHICLES

Beyond transporting agents from point A to point B, CTU-equipped vehicles can serve as a staging center for tactical ops when larger mobile command stations are not an option. Vehicles are bulletproof and can provide temporary shelter when under fire. All CTU vehicles are equipped with an onboard computer, including a flatbed scanner with both optical and magnetic capabilities, and GPS tracking with satellite uplink capabilities.

080
079
078
077
076
075
074
073
072
071
070
069
068
067
066
065
064
063
062
061
060
059
058
057
056
055
054
053
052

SUPPLY CHECKLIST

The following items are recommended by CTU. Before deployment, verify that these items are on hand, either in the vehicle or on your person:

- Balaclava (per agent)
- Battering ram
- Flaregun/flares
- Floodlight
- Full locksmith kit
- Gas masks (depending on mission)
- Grenades
- Handheld flashlight (per agent)
- Handheld PDA/cell phone with GPS capability (per agent)
- Handheld two-way (per agent)
- Mirror with extendable shaft
- Night-vision goggles (depending on mission)
- Night-vision monocular or "scope" (for night ops)

- Plastic explosives (C4 or other)
- Spotting scopes (per agent)
- Standard CTU-issue first-aid kit, including
  - Smelling salts
  - Epinephrine injection
  - Suicide capsules (Not standard issue in tactical first-aid kits.)
- Standard handcuffs (per agent)
- Surveillance package
- Tactical ear (per agent)
- Tactical knives (per agent)
- Tasers and stun guns
- Tear gas
- Tranquilizer gun (depending on mission)
- Weapons package*

*For CTU-approved firearms, see detailed list in section B2.

081

080

079

078

077

076

075

074

073

072

071

070

069

068

067

066

065

064

063

062

061

060

059

058

YOUR MESSENGER BAG

Individual agents in the field, whether they have gone dark or are simply traveling on foot and need to remain mobile, must operate effectively without the benefit of a full CTU arsenal. In the past, agents such as Jack Bauer have been forced to survive with whatever they can fit in their dependable military messenger bags. Must-haves include:

- 9mm semi-automatic pistols (2)
- Ace bandage
- Alternate identification (passport, license, etc.)
- Aspirin
- Batteries: extra for cell phone and PDA
- Charger: for cell phone and PDA
- Disposable plastic restraints: lightweight and useful for handcuffing on the go
- Duct tape
- Extra magazines: as many as you can carry, since you may not be able to stock up frequently
- Fisher Space Pen
- Flash drive (5GB)
- Handheld PDA and cell phone with GPS capabilities

- Instant cold compress
- Latex gloves
- Lockmith's pick set
- Magnetic compass
- Matches, lighter
- Microtech H.A.L.O. tactical knife
- Mini-flashlight
- Polarized sunglasses
- Small mirror with extendable shaft
- Spotting scope
- Sterile gauze
- Stun gun
- Swiss army knife
- Ziploc bags

082
081
080
079
078
077
076
075
074
073
072
071
070
069
068
067
066
065
064
063
062
061
060
059
058
057
056
055
054

53

WHEN YOU'RE ON THE MOVE, A SIMPLE, DURABLE MESSENGER BAG CAN HOLD ALL OF YOUR ESSENTIAL GEAR.

083
082
081
080
079
078
077
076
075
074
073
072
071
070
069
068
067
066
065
064
063
062
061
060
059
058
057
056
055
54

083
082
081
080
079
078
077
076
075
074
073
072
071
070
069
068
067
066
065
064
063
062
061
060
059
058
057
056

B2 — APPROVED FIREARMS FOR CTU AGENTS

CTU provides firearms and weaponry training. All agents—whether field or intelligence—are required to pass CTU firearms proficiency testing for handguns and assault rifles, despite prior certifications or training at other organizations. If you are currently certified by CTU in both handguns and assault rifles but would like to undertake sniper training, speak to your supervisor; he or she can help you begin the qualification process. Keep in mind that sniper training is extremely intense. It requires a degree of marksmanship and psychological skill that not everyone—even some of the best agents—possesses.

SNIPER RIFLES

Standard sniper rifle issue at CTU is the PSG-1 semi-automatic, which has proved to be preferable in urban settings. It provides enhanced accuracy over shorter ranges when compared to the military-issue M40A3.

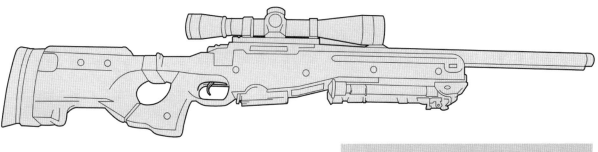

PSG-1 SNIPER RIFLE

ASSAULT RIFLES

The M4 carbine configured to mission specs may include detachable grenade launcher, infrared illuminator, night-vision sight, and visible laser. The M4 has proved to be very reliable. It was used on Day 4 in a siege jointly staged by CTU and U.S. Marines to liberate Secretary of Defense James Heller and his daughter Audrey Raines when they were held captive by terrorists at a well-guarded compound.

085
084
083
082
081
080
079
078
077
076
075
074
073
072
071
070
069
068
067
066
065
064
063
062
061
060
059
058
057

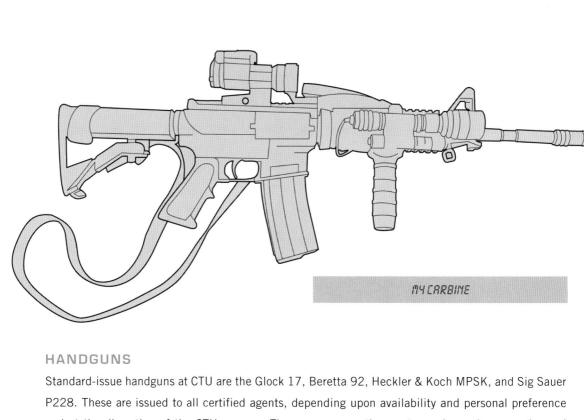

M4 CARBINE

HANDGUNS

Standard-issue handguns at CTU are the Glock 17, Beretta 92, Heckler & Koch MPSK, and Sig Sauer P228. These are issued to all certified agents, depending upon availability and personal preference and at the discretion of the CTU armorer. These are among the most popular and commonly used handguns by law enforcement agencies worldwide. You will find ammunition easily available if you are forced to improvise on a mission.

If your mission requires a sound-suppressor package, make the armorer aware of this need, and the appropriate suppressor-modified tactical weapon will be issued.

HECKLER & KOCH MPSK

SIG SAUER P228

086
085
084
083
082
081
080
079
078
077
076
075
074
073

TERRORIST VLADIMIR BIERKO
USED SENTOX VX NERVE GAS AS
HIS WEAPON OF CHOICE.

072
071
070
069
068
067
066
065
064
063
062
061
060
059
058

B3

UNDERSTANDING THE TERRORIST ARSENAL

The terrorists that CTU fights all day, every day, are both amply supplied and highly motivated. Some of their weapons are the same as our own. For the purposes of this manual, we highlight those weapons that terrorists use to instill fear in the populace. These are devices that either cause pandemonium and chaos or harm large numbers of innocent people—or both. Many are weapons that no U.S. agency would ever use, especially in urban areas. Individuals in positions of power, misguided by a distorted sense of ambition and a twisted concept of patriotism—such as disgraced former president Charles Logan—find ways to justify supplying terrorists with these kinds of weapons. We need to know how to respond to them to keep Americans out of harm's way.

087
086
085
084
083
082
081
080
079
078
077
076
75
074
073
072
071
070
069
068
067
066
065
064
063
062
061
060
059
5A

THIS EMP BOMB WAS DETONATED ON DAY 4 AND DESTROYED ALL ELECTRONIC DEVICES WITHIN AN EIGHT-MILE RADIUS.

ELECTRO-MAGNETIC PULSE (EMP) BOMBS

To seriously cripple a society, terrorists often strike at its infrastructure. That is exactly what is accomplished with an electromagnetic pulse bomb or "E-bomb." The high-density electromagnetic field that results from the detonation of an E-bomb can wipe out all electronic devices within a substantial range. EMPs are also a serious consequence of the detonation of a nuclear bomb, even those detonated hundreds of miles above Earth's surface. Although EMPs may not harm people, the systems and information they destroy can derail lives and investigations. EMPs have been used by private-sector security forces to secure—or rather, eliminate—incriminating information. This tactic was employed on Day 4 by military contractor McClennan-Forster, which had not only developed the Dobson Override but was also developing EMPs for the military. The detonation of an EMP bomb on its own premises was an effort to destroy files linking the corporation to terrorist Habib Marwan. Unfortunately, the damage was not limited to their organization; it took out all systems within an eight-mile radius. Luckily, CTU's overall mission was successful that day. But the havoc the EMP wreaked was not forgotten, and weapons of this kind remain a very real and serious threat.

088
087
086
085
084
083
082
081
080
079
078
077
076
075
074
073
072
071
070
069
068
067
066
065
064
063
062
061
060

SENTOX NERVE GAS

Sentox is a VX nerve agent manufactured both legally and illegally by companies in various parts of the world, including the U.S. military contractor Omicron International. The first VX-class nerve agents were developed in the 1950s and have the lowest lethal dosage of all nerve agents: They can kill in a matter of minutes if inhaled or touched to the skin. Nerve agents disrupt the functioning of important enzymes in the nervous system that regulate acetylcholine levels. The drug atropine is a viable treatment for exposure; it doesn't attack the nerve gas but helps minimize the effects of excess acetylcholine and can be used to keep a victim functioning until the substance has worked its way out of the system.

BIOWEAPONS

To date, the most dangerous bioweapon ever used on a civilian population on American soil is the Cordilla virus, which was released by terrorists led by former British intelligence agent Stephen Saunders on Day 3. It resulted in the quarantine of the Chandler Plaza Hotel and at least 800 deaths. A Type III—high-priority—pneumonic virus, the Cordilla belongs to the class of immuno-pulmonary viruses. In a weaponized state, it has an incubation period of fourteen hours, after which time hosts begin to exhibit symptoms such as nose bleeds and skin sores. Once symptomatic, hosts are highly contagious, and death occurs within twenty-four hours. In the attack on the Chandler, terrorists used a version of the Cordilla virus developed by Marcus Alvers that produced an accelerated progression of this

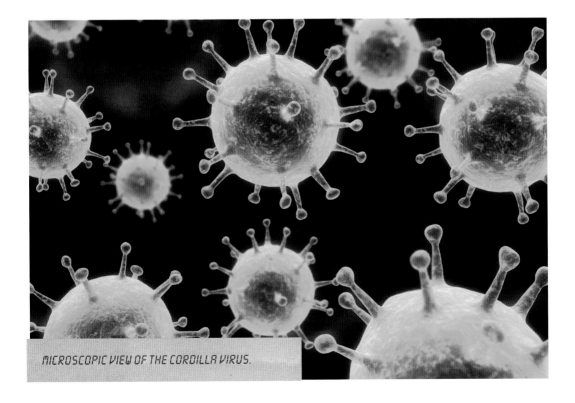

MICROSCOPIC VIEW OF THE CORDILLA VIRUS.

089
088
087
086
085
084
083
082
081
080
079
078
077
076
075
074
073
072
071
070
069
068
067
066
065
064
063
062
061

biological disease. Such an outcome demonstrates that a familiar substance in dangerous hands can result in an even more powerful weapon.

ROCKET-PROPELLED GRENADES (RPG)

Highly practical for attacks on cars and buildings, RPGs are often used by terrorists who favor the shoulder-launching capabilities of these weapons to immobilize moving vehicles. Few vehicles—even bulletproof ones—are a match for a direct hit from an RPG. Terrorists employed these to attack the bulletproof vehicle of Defense Secretary Heller on Day 4, after he insisted on visiting his son Richard, and the motorcade of the Russian president Suvarov traveling to the airport on Day 5.

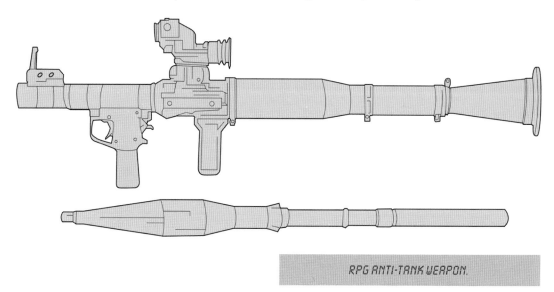

RPG ANTI-TANK WEAPON.

"DIRTY BOMB" OR RADIOLOGICAL DISPERSAL DEVICE (RDD)

Although not highly sophisticated, dirty bombs are crude weapons that combine a basic explosive with a radioactive substance. They are *not* nuclear bombs. The lethality of the RDD depends on whether it contains weapons-grade isotopes. Depending on the kind of radioactive material, more damage may be caused by the explosion itself than by the nuclear substance. However, if a potent radioactive material is used, several city blocks may be contaminated. Fortunately, many of the more dangerous materials—including Strontium-90—are often the most difficult to find and handle safely. Nevertheless, the devices are very easy to make and therefore pose a threat. A terrorist with access to high-grade radioactive material is of great concern. Regardless of how lethal the weapon is, the panic it causes poses a true danger. The detonation of a dirty-bomb can result in mass hysteria, rampant fear, and subsequent chaos. CTU agents dispatched to the scene of a dirty-bomb detonation should work with local law enforcement to employ standard crowd-control techniques. (For more on handling these situations, see section G, "Disaster Management.")

090

089

088

087

086

085

084

083

082

081

080

079

078

077

076

075

074

073

072

071

070

069

068

067

066

065

064

063

062

SUITCASE NUKE

Terrorists often have to travel light, and the ability to contain a nuclear device in a suitcase fits their mission objectives perfectly. Such small-scale weapons can be carried onto public transportation, left in a train station locker, stowed under a bus seat, and the like. When nuclear devices are decommissioned, they are often dismantled, and the pieces can be stored and transported separately to a new location to be reconfigured with new trigger mechanisms. They are therefore more difficult to track, even if they are less powerful than their larger counterparts. The suitcase nuke detonated on Day 6, for example, killed approximately 12,000 (though more died from the after-effects of the radioactivity). Although this sum is not insignificant, it pales in comparison to the casualties that would result from the detonation of a full-size nuclear warhead. But what these devices lack in destructive capability, they make up for in portability and ease of concealment.

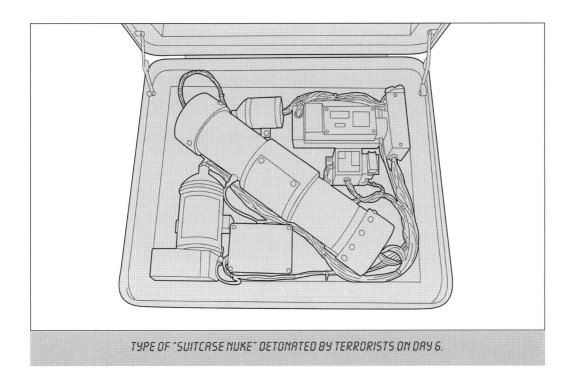

TYPE OF "SUITCASE NUKE" DETONATED BY TERRORISTS ON DAY 6.

CYANIDE PILLS

Be aware that almost all terrorist operatives are willing to die for their cause. For this reason, many of them carry cyanide pills at all times and will ingest them as soon as they believe that their being taken alive is a possibility. When apprehending suspects, watch to be sure they have not attempted to place anything in their mouths or bite down hard (some capsules are embedded in false teeth); otherwise their lives—and your intel-gathering—will soon be over.

089
088
087
086
085
084
083
082
081
080
079
078
077
076
075
074
073
072
071
070
069

I M P O R T A N T

Dangerous devices can be created from seemingly harmless and readily available objects and ingredients. Common bug spray and other pesticides can serve as nerve agents. Hospitals use, and regularly dispose of, radioactive materials. Flamethrowers can be fashioned from hairspray and a lighted match. The traitor Nina Myers once used a torn plastic card to cut the throat of a fellow conspirator. In other words: Stay alert.

THE ART OF DIVERSION

CTU agents have many techniques and technologies at their disposal. However, little can compare to keen insight. Terrorists know the importance of the element of surprise in warfare. They master the art of diversion to throw law enforcement agencies off their scent. By occupying agencies with a "crisis"—such as the kidnapping of the Secretary of Defense—they manage to mask a larger, more threatening objective and, in the process, divert valuable resources that might stop them from achieving it. Agents should never take situations at face value, even when they are knee-deep in response to a serious state of affairs. Examples abound throughout CTU history. Consider the bombing of CTU on Day 2. Though we all were devastated by the loss of our colleagues and friends, the real threat—an armed nuclear warhead and the possibility of World War III—had yet to be revealed. We acknowledge that it can be difficult to remain detached, but we cannot emphasize enough that *remaining detached is your job.* If, under any circumstances, you are having difficulty remaining objective on the job, do yourself, your colleagues, and the citizens of the United States a favor: Seek counseling from the CTU psychologist on call. All consultations with CTU psychologists remain confidential unless an agent's overall mental health is determined to threaten the security and safety of CTU.

C | SURVEILLANCE

THE COUNTER TERRORIST UNIT MUST BE ABLE TO MOBILIZE AND SPRING INTO ACTION AT A MOMENT'S NOTICE. NEVERTHELESS, A SIGNIFICANT PART OF WHAT WE DO IS OBSERVE, WATCH, AND LEARN. AT ANY GIVEN TIME, WE ARE MONITORING SCORES OF HOSTILES—THOSE WHO ARE ACTIVELY ENGAGED IN A CURRENT TERRORIST ATTACK AND THOSE WHO ARE MERELY ONGOING SUBJECTS OF MONTHLY, WEEKLY, OR EVEN DAILY SCRUTINY. THE LATTER MAY SOMEDAY PROVIDE THE INFORMATION WE NEED TO BRING DOWN A TERRORIST ORGANIZATION.

095
094
093
092
091
090
089
088
087
086
085
084
083
082
081
080
079
078
077
076
075
074
073
072
071
070
069
068
067

It goes without saying that these are highly organized groups, and dropping in on their activities at a time of crisis does not provide nearly enough intelligence for our purposes. We watch them as well as their families, businesses, and known associates. We may track individuals for months or even years, and the target's archived activity—including satellite images—can provide us with a comprehensive picture that will enable us to better bring down the hostiles or their organization when time is of the essence. And it always is.

In past decades, effective target surveillance was accomplished with equipment that may appear dated and even obsolete compared with today's technology. Do not underestimate the importance of these techniques. It's true that we now rely on devices as large as a satellite or as minuscule as a micro-transmitter. These are all extraordinarily powerful devices, but they also have limitations. No technique or equipment is foolproof. None will work in all situations. Technology can be turned against you and can also be thwarted by adversaries who understand how it functions.

A good agent knows what to use and when to use it and understands how to weigh the benefits and limitations of a surveillance approach. Most important, agents should always keep in mind that "low-tech" is sometimes the best way to catch a subject off-guard.

OVERVIEW OF SATELLITE SURVEILLANCE SYSTEMS

Increasingly, surveillance of hostiles and the monitoring of our own field agents rely on satellites. A nuts-and-bolts discussion of this technology is beyond the scope of this document. Suffice it to say that our government has gone to great expense to embed a vast network of satellites in orbit around Earth. Typically, satellites have a benign commercial purpose and are thus employed in every facet of American life. They make possible the use of cell phones, televisions, and other electronic communications. They are efficient conduits for the transmission of information from one location to another on the other side of the planet.

At the same time, some satellites—the precise number and function of which are classified—are employed for mission-critical surveillance by key gov-

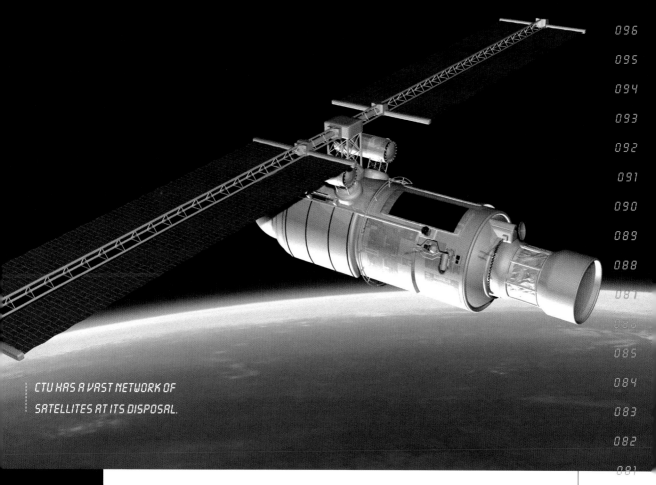

096
095
094
093
092
091
090
089
088
087
086
085
084
083
082
081

CTU HAS A VAST NETWORK OF
SATELLITES AT ITS DISPOSAL.

080
079
078
077
076
075
074
073
072
071
070
069
068

ernment agencies, CTU among them. Endowed with powerful optics, a typical "keyhole" satellite can observe and capture images of objects approximately six inches or larger from miles above the Earth's surface. Agents on the floor can track not only a hostile's vehicle but also his handling of his suitcase, PDA, weapon, and mobile phone. When combined with global positioning systems (GPS), which also relay data via satellite, these can be impressive surveillance tools.

Be aware that satellite coverage, although expensive, cannot track every area on the planet at every moment of the day. You may also find that sometimes resolution can be "noisy." While CTU does have redundant satellite coverage of certain locales, we do not have our own dedicated satellite.

Surveillance use of U.S. satellites generally falls into two major categories: digital imaging and infrared imaging.

097
096
095
094
093
092
091
090
089
088
087
086
085
084
083
082
081
080
079
078
077
076
075
074
073
072
071
070
069

DIGITAL SATELLITE IMAGING

An intelligence agent armed with the correct longitude and latitude, the precise time of an event, and proper clearance from his or her supervisor can access files of images captured by a U.S. satellite minutes, hours, days, or even months in the past. With proper clearance it is also possible to capture and view real-time video of an event on Earth's surface. In general, we use this type of imaging to observe hostile subjects walking on the ground, driving a vehicle, or engaged in outdoor or public activities day or night.

This satellite technology is fast becoming the best way to track a suspect in a vehicle. Where a satellite cannot be used due to a lack of interagency cooperation, momentary malfunction, or data corruption or deletion, intelligence agents can obtain visuals from local traffic cameras. (For more on traffic cameras, see section C3, page 80.)

A SATELLITE IMAGE OF GENEVA, SWITZERLAND.

INFRARED SATELLITE IMAGING

Some satellites are equipped with infrared imaging optics. This technology allows them to pick up the specific heat signature radiated by life forms and high-heat-emitting devices, such as activated missiles, bombs, or other equipment. A real-time infrared image, for example, will allow you to observe hostiles moving about inside a structure day or night. Remember: This technology is useless for identifying suspects because you are viewing a heat signature, not a photograph. It is extremely useful if you are moving on a guarded compound and need to know the number and location of hostiles present, both inside and around the structure(s).

For all their advantages, however, satellites are not perfect. They look straight down at Earth, which often makes it impossible to capture images suitable for biometric, or facial recognition, analysis. Our success in this area depends on the subject looking up, which is rare. Other imaging devices, such as a hand-held camera, pole-mounted traffic camera, or closed-circuit security camera, can often be more helpful in obtaining pictures of a hostile's face.

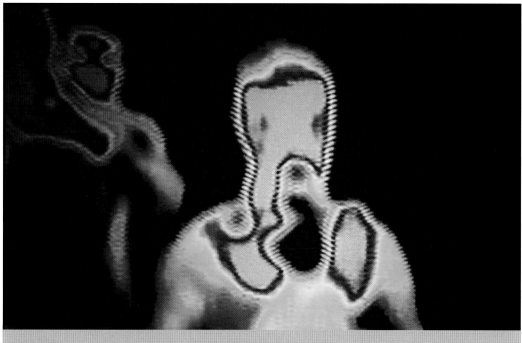

INFRARED IMAGING CAN REVEAL THE HEAT SIGNATURE OF VARIOUS LIFE FORMS.

I M P O R T A N T

Senior analysts and intelligence agents specializing in satellite tracking are the key points of contact on sensitive missions. You must gain permission from your CTU SAC or deputy director before commencing satellite tracking. We do not have a dedicated satellite reserved for our exclusive use. Any agent who accesses a satellite, decrypts archived satellite images, or steals bandwidth from another agency's satellite requisition without prior approval from a supervisor faces suspension and/or arrest. We realize that every government agency believes its mission has priority, but we cannot condone this behavior; it jeopardizes CTU's relationship with other agencies. Although the end may seem to justify the means, you are taking your career—and perhaps your freedom—

098
097
096
095
094
093
092
091
090
089
088
087
086
085
084
083
082
081
080
079
078
077
076
075
074
073
072
071
070

099
098
097
096
095
094
093
092
091
090
089
088
087
086
085

AGENTS FOUND STEALING SATELLITE SURVEILLANCE BANDWIDTH MAY FACE CRIMINAL INVESTIGATION.

081
080
079
078
077
076
075
074
073
072
071

into your own hands. No matter what the results, unauthorized satellite usage will not go unnoticed and will be reflected in your personnel file as long as you are employed at CTU.

Recall the actions of Agent O'Brian on Day 4, when she effectively stole CTU satellite surveillance bandwith to help Agent Bauer track suspect Kalil Hasan in hopes of locating the compound where terrorists were holding Defense Secretary Heller and Audrey Raines. Though the mission was eventually a success, Agent O'Brian's actions deviated from standard CTU operating procedures, and this offense was noted in her dossier.

100
099
098
097
096
095
094
093
092
091
090
089
088
087
086
085
084
083
082
081
080
079
078
077
076
075
074
073
072

OVERVIEW OF OTHER TRACKING AND SURVEILLANCE DEVICES

Knowing what targets are doing, where they're operating, and with whom they're working is key to the success of any mission. CTU may access the most advanced tracking devices available, many of which are accessible only to military or governmental operations with proper clearance. Tracking devices are available in many shapes and sizes: a tiny microtransmitter can be placed on the cap of a fountain pen, cameras in buttonholes, and transponders in automobile-wheel wells.

Some of the techniques below have been instrumental not only in stopping terrorist activity but also in saving the lives of field agents. For tracking to be effective, however, the devices must be put into play. Doing so often requires getting up close and personal with the targets themselves, their contacts, or their equipment.

TRACK HOSTILES

to lead you to their contacts and command centers is a valuable technique and one that inking to put into action. Successful execution requires that you know your target's psy-nticipate his or her moves.

THEM THINK THEY'VE GOTTEN AWAY. The ideal way to track hostiles is, obviously, so without their knowing. You want the targets to remain comfortable and to let their down. Let them think they've given you the slip, so they won't be worried that you're fol-g them. Make them believe they have the upper hand. Their confidence can be used to advantage—a big ego is usually a big weakness.

The best example in recent CTU history occurred on Day 3 during the tracking of Cordilla salesman Michael Amador. When Agents Bauer and Edmunds successfully tracked dor to a Chinatown nightclub, they proceeded to interrogate him. In the process, Agent

101
100
099
098
097
096
095
094
093
092
091
090
089
088
087
086
085
084

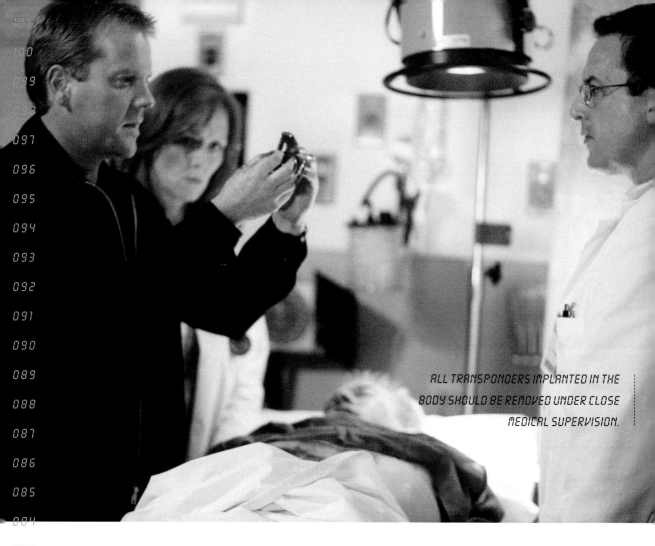

ALL TRANSPONDERS IMPLANTED IN THE BODY SHOULD BE REMOVED UNDER CLOSE MEDICAL SUPERVISION.

083
082
081
080
079
078
077
076
075
074
073

Edmunds sliced Amador's hand with a knife. A transponder was placed in the bandage used to wrap the hand, after which Amador was cuffed to a less-than-stable radiator. When Amador "escaped," CTU was able to track him because he was convinced that he was not being followed, right up until the detonation of the briefcase bomb that abruptly ended his life.

PLACE THE TRACKING DEVICE IN A LOCATION THEY WON'T SUSPECT AND DO SO WHEN THEY LEAST SUSPECT IT. Hostiles are just as aware as any agent of the possibility that their movements may be tracked and their objectives compromised. Getting to them when their guard is down is crucial. Take advantage of any occasion when the hostile is incapacitated. Sometimes this tactic works, sometimes it does not. For example, on Day 1, Alexis Drazen was stabbed by Elizabeth Nash, David Palmer's campaign aide, and was subsequently hospitalized. That presented the perfect opportunity to implant a transponder on his hospital bracelet. This made exchanging Drazen for Agent Bauer an opportunity to track the Drazen family movements.

Unfortunately, the limitations of such a tracking device—namely, that it can be revealed by a signal detector—meant the wristband was destroyed before it could be put to much use by CTU.

USE MULTIPLE DEVICES, INCLUDING A DECOY. Always consider planting multiple devices, including one that is meant to be found. In some cases, a target working fast and under pressure will stop sweeping for signals once the first and most obvious device is located. Agents should also keep this point in mind when sweeping for signals. Remember to ask yourself: Is this bug the one they wanted me to find?

TRACK SOMEONE CLOSE TO THE TARGET, RATHER THAN THE ACTUAL TARGET. Ankle bracelets are commonly used for individuals under house arrest, but they can also track someone currently under arrest who has agreed to cooperate with the agency. Suspects—such as CTU mole Marianne Taylor—wearing an ankle bracelet interact with their contacts and can easily access locations and information that CTU agents could not. Again, this strategy should be employed only if the target will not be actively sweeping the insider for bugs. It is not guaranteed, but the target is less likely to sweep someone they know and trust. This technique is most effective if implemented quickly, before the target has time to learn that his or her contact has been compromised.

TRACKING AGENTS

CTU agents take great risks when undercover. Tracking devices usually help minimize these risks. Undercover field agents often do not have the option of using their PDA or CTU-issued cell phone to establish position. When choosing a tracking device, jewelry can be more effective than clothing since it will not raise suspicion if worn on consecutive days. In fact, on Day 3, when Agent Bauer reestablished his cover with the Salazar crime organization in Las Nieves, Mexico, he used a wristwatch device that allowed CTU to track his position. Unfortunately, Bauer's watch was damaged, rendering it useless. If tracking devices are compromised, remember that you are on your own, especially if satellite coverage or other GPS tracking is limited or unavailable.

INVASIVE TRACKING

Tracking devices can also be implanted beneath the skin. These microtracking devices are embedded with minimal pain, though some discomfort is experienced, and will emit a homing beacon picked up by global positioning satellites. Again, this approach is not foolproof. Any device that emits a signal—whether implanted or worn externally—can be revealed. That was exactly the case on Day 4, when Behrooz Araz—son of known terrorists Navi and Dina Araz—had a tracking device implanted in the nape of his neck before he was traded to Habib Marwan in exchange for Agent Bauer. The diligence of the terrorists revealed the location of the implanted bug, and it was successfully—and painfully—excised from Araz and thus rendered ineffective.

GPS TRACKING

Cell phones and PDAs can easily be tracked using the global positioning satellite network. Many field agents often use their PDAs to relay their position to CTU. Even cell phones that are turned off can still be tracked using passive triangulation. As a backup to satellite tracking, GPS transponders can also be used to track automobiles, provided that the vehicle has not been swept.

BUGGING CONVERSATIONS AND ROOMS

Traditional telephone and room bugging is also a tried-and-true way to listen in on a target's conversations and monitor the target's activities, provided that you can gain advance access to a site where such conversations/activities will occur. Fiber-optic cameras may be inserted through tiny crevices in the walls of a building, and the activities can then be monitored from an adjacent room or off-site.

HELICOPTERS MAY BE USED TO TRAIL A SUSPECT, BUT THEY ARE HARDLY DISCREET.

101
100
099
098
097
096
095
094
093
092
091
090
089
088
087
086
085
084
083
082
081
080
079
078
077
076

105
104
103
102
101
100
099
098
097
096
095
094
093
092
091
090
089
088
087
086
085
084
083
082
081
080
079
078
077

LISTENING TO CELL PHONE CONVERSATIONS

Many phone calls—made from land lines or cellular phones—can be tracked, but this type of surveillance allows you to listen to conversations only if you have had access to the equipment. Of course, government agencies have the ability to listen to conversations much more easily than the average citizen, though the use of these technologies is not always considered legal and has been recently challenged in the courts and debated in the media. Alternate methods of gaining access to cell phone conversations exist as well. It was once common for electronic serial numbers (ESN) and mobile identification numbers (MIN) to be compromised and used to "clone" an individual's cellular account. However, if you can gain access to an unsuspecting target's actual cell phone, you can now use it to activate a "listen-in." Defense Secretary Heller's son Richard was the unsuspecting victim of a listen-in tactic. After being picked up at a bar and bringing his new "friends" back to his place, he did not anticipate that his cell phone could be used against his family. Yet in just the few moments he was away from his phone, the terrorists were able to activate the listen-in. The professional assassin-for-hire, known only as "Mandy," used the opportunity to place a call to Habib Marwan from the phone and then allowed Marwan to listen to all the calls that took place between Richard Heller and his father. It also later implicated Richard in the kidnapping and conspiracy.

RECORDING AUDIO WITH MICROTRANSMITTERS

A wide variety of microtransmitters can be used to effectively record conversations. This strategy was most notably used in the regrettable—but necessary—apprehension of former president Charles Logan. During the capture and interrogation of Logan, Agent Bauer was able to plant a microtransmitter on the president's Mont Blanc pen. Bauer knew that Logan would confess nothing to him; when Bauer allowed himself to be captured, he accomplished an important feat: He made the president feel comfortable, as though Agent Bauer had been bested. When Logan later confronted the First Lady at the airfield where David Palmer's body was about to be flown home for burial, Logan's suspicion and paranoia were focused on his surroundings and his wife. He overlooked the possibility that he had been bugged.

LET OTHERS DO YOUR WORK FOR YOU

Security cameras are everywhere, from ATMs and convenience stores to traffic cameras and hospitals. Use footage that others have already gathered to supplement your own real-time tracking. Your supervisors on the floor can coach you through your first use of this approach and apprise you of the various types of equipment operated by other agencies and organizations that might be useful to your mission.

ON DAY 5, AGENT JACK BAUER AND FIRST LADY MARTHA LOGAN "BUGGED" PRESIDENT CHARLES LOGAN USING A TRANSMITTER HIDDEN IN A MONT BLANC PEN.

108
109
104
103
102
101
100
099
098
097
096
095
094
093
092

091

090

089

088

087

086

085

084

083

082

081

080

079

078

107
106
105
104
103
102
101
100
099
098
097
096
095
094
093
092
091
090
089
088
087
086
085
084
083
082
081
080
079
78

LOW-TECH SURVEILLANCE

The ability to study a target's activities, movements, and habits with the naked eye often provides better clues to his thinking than can eye-in-the-sky observation. Moreover, if you know your target is likely to sweep for implanted tracking devices, "passive" surveillance is the only option. Speak to your supervisor about initiating the use of mobile parabolics. This technology—characterized by the use of a powerful microphone nested in a handheld, 20-inch dish—can amplify and record real-time conversations taking place up to 300 yards away. The technology is better than a standard shotgun microphone, though it, too, has limitations. For one thing, it sticks out like a sore thumb and must maintain line of sight at all times to function properly. Use only when you know or believe field agents employing the device are unlikely to be observed. If doing so seems risky, switch to a wireless, unidirectional microphone, which may be concealed in a broadsheet newspaper or large magazine. In this manner, a series of undercover agents dispersed throughout an open setting, for example, can follow a target and capture ongoing audio without interruption or attracting unwanted attention.

C3

HOW TO TRAIL A SUSPECT WITHOUT BEING DETECTED

Trailing or "tailing" a suspect is one of the most important, yet thankless, tasks you will ever tackle at CTU. Leaders of terrorist organizations know they are too valuable to come out of hiding, so they remain in seclusion and send less-important operatives to do their bidding. With some skill and preparation, you can follow an underling back to a leader's command center, take down the architect of the organization, and dismantle his arsenal.

Getting there, however, is rarely easy. Trailing is challenging because suspects may access multiple modes of transportation. If you are trailing a suspect in a pedestrian setting—a park, a "walkable" city, a mall—you can easily keep up on foot. However, if he hails a cab, hops a bus, or hot-wires a car, you will quickly lose him if you are unprepared.

108
107
106
105
104
103
102
101
100
099
098
097
096
095
094
093
092
091
090
089
088
087
086
085
084
083
082
081
080

Therefore, we recommend that no fewer than three agents be involved in a tail job. It is much more difficult for a single agent to tail a suspect because no one individual can be prepared for all the modes of travel available to a terrorist, especially one with great financial resources. If the suspect is in a vehicle, we recommend that at least three agents follow in three separate vehicles. We recognize that CTU missions develop on the fly and may not permit such redundant tracking. In an ideal scenario, another three agents should be on standby, ready to assume watch in a pedestrian setting, to "cover" by air via helicopter, or to access other necessary transportation modes.

Since vehicle tails will probably be the most common types conducted by CTU agents, we will discuss them almost exclusively. The following suggestions will help you keep a suspect in your sights.

AVOID SIMILAR MOVEMENTS.

Even if you are tailing a suspect from three or four car lengths, this person will spot you if you persist in maneuvering your vehicle to mimic his or her every move. If the suspect moves to the right lane, stay where you are. You can always move later, if the situation warrants. Otherwise, stay put. All you need to maintain surveillance is a constant visual of the suspect.

BE MINDFUL OF UPCOMING TRAFFIC CHOICES.

If you stay fixed in the left lane, you will lose the suspect if he or she makes a sudden right onto an exit ramp. Stay alert to all the available "outs." The suspect can exit the road, veer into oncoming traffic, hide in an alley or driveway, or ditch the vehicle and take off on foot. If you are not prepared for these surprises, you will be unable to move quickly when they occur.

USE A DECOY.

In cases where the suspect tends to be suspicious of his or her surroundings, it helps to create a false sense of confidence by using a "decoy tail." In this scenario, one agent follows the suspect in a very obvious manner, by driving too close to the suspect, by conspicuously talking on a cell phone, or by pretending to talk into a handset. The suspect's suspicions quickly become aroused, and he or she does something to shake the tail, such as reverse direction, exit the freeway, or switch vehicles. The decoy tail acts confused, then disappears from the suspect's line of vision, giving the impression that the sus-

109
108
107
106
105
104
103
102
101
100
099
098
097
096
095
094
093
092
091
090
089
088
087
086
085
084
083
082
081

pect has successfully lost the tail. What the suspect does not know is that one or more agents are continuing to follow at a distance. Indeed, this person has never left their sights.

WORK THE PARALLEL ROADS.

If you are working closely with the floor at CTU, you will be able to take advantage of satellite tracking while pursuing a subject. Satellite imaging allows CTU to advise you of parallel roads where you can remain unseen while following the subject. Your SAC and intelligence agent will be able to advise you of your options. Even though you are on a different road, it pays to stay a safe distance behind the suspect. You don't want to reveal your location if you are spotted at a cross street.

I M P O R T A N T

The intelligence agent assigned to your case has a view of the situation that you do not. He or she will know if the suspect has changed course one-half mile ahead of you and out of your sight range. If you have begun tailing a suspect without advance warning, contact the floor as soon as possible to see if satellite coverage is available in your location.

Use alternate technology wherever possible. Satellite surveillance is not your only option. The California Department of Transportation maintains hundreds of cameras throughout the city and county, covering both freeways and surface roads. Ostensibly, these are not to be used by law-enforcement agencies. However, a simple covert work-around can get you into the system when necessary. (Speak to your supervisor or SAC for details.) Caltrans traffic cameras can help with difficult angles, spotting license plates, and nailing down details that cannot be observed by satellite or would simply take too long to analyze with image enhancement. Early on Day 3, Analysts Kim Bauer and Adam Kaufman were able to track teenager Kyle Singer and his girlfriend Linda, who were abducted by terrorists. By studying Caltrans images, Bauer and Kaufman observed the blue shirt worn by the missing teen, as seen through the window of the terrorists' truck, as well as the gun being pointed at his side. This type of detail could come only from a camera trained close to the ground, as opposed to a satellite.

Know when to stop and call for backup. Chances are great that the closer the subject gets to his HQ, the more deserted the neighborhood will become, and thus the more obvious your movements or presence. You must cultivate a good sense for knowing when to stop trailing your suspect. That does not mean you should stop working the tail. It means you park or obscure your vehicle in a safe location and await backup from CTU's tactical team. In some cases, you will be expected to maintain a visual on the terrorist hideout, if the terrain permits. Only in the most crit-

110
109
108
107
106
105
104
103
102
101
100

099
098
097
096
095
094
093
092
091

ical circumstances—and with full CTU approval— would you attempt to storm the terrorist HQ on your own. During the tense moments of Day 4 when Secretary of Defense James Heller and his daughter

CALTRANS TRAFFIC CAMERAS ARE AN EXCELLENT ALTERNATIVE TO SATELLITE SURVEILLANCE.

Audrey Raines were being held hostage by a group of radicals, Agent Bauer ignored CTU's instructions to leave the area outside the terrorists' facility and prepare for airborne attack. Instead, with U.S. Marine support, Bauer stormed the facility, killed twelve terrorists, and ultimately rescued Secretary Heller and Ms. Raines. Though this mission was successful, new recruits are reminded that it could easily have gone the other way. *Do not* circumvent CTU authority, no matter how passionate you feel about the way your mission should be handled.

090
089
088
087
086
085
084
083
082

C4   HOW TO TELL IF YOU'RE BEING TRAILED

Contrary to common perception, terrorists have vastly different motives for following CTU agents than we have for following them. We tail to locate a group's leaders, identify dangerous stockpiles of weapons, rescue innocent civilians and important individuals who may have been abducted, and take the hostiles into custody to extract further information. Unfortunately, if they're on your tail, they may be trying to abduct or kill you. That's why

111
110
109
108
107
106
105
104
103
102
101
100
099
098
097
096
095
094
093
092
091
090
089
088
087
086
085
084
083

you must be able to tell if you are the subject of a tail job. It could cost you your life. Here are some tips for identifying and dealing with a vehicle tail.

1. TRUST YOUR GUT.

Chances are if you think you're being trailed, you probably are. Your gut is picking up on clues ignored by your rational mind. Tune in. Unlike you, the terrorists may not have been schooled in surveillance techniques. Their amateurish behavior will likely give them away. Scan your rearview mirror, then the side mirrors, and mentally note the cars behind you and to your sides. Do you recognize any? Is anyone behaving suspiciously? Are they driving too fast? Too slow? Are they cutting through two or more lanes to get into yours? Does anyone appear to be preoccupied with an object below the dashboard level? It could be a weapon. Keep your eye on these vehicles—and the road.

2. REVIEW YOUR MISSION AND ASSESS THE THREAT.

Before you can take action, figure out why you have been singled out for this special attention. Recall the facts of your mission and decide the most likely reason that you are being trailed. Sometimes it will be obvious—other times, less so. Put yourself in the mind of the person you believe to be following you: Do you have something the hostiles want? What events have occurred in the last sixty minutes pertaining to your mission? If you are off-duty and not on a mission, consider the possibility that you are being trailed because you are expected to lead the hostiles to a friend or family member. Perform this mental review quickly; it will determine your next action.

3. PRACTICE VEHICULAR EVASION (ON SURFACE ROADS).

This maneuver boils down to a game of driving skills. Thanks to thirty-plus hours with CTU driving instructors, you have it and they don't. To sniff them out, switch lanes once or twice to see if anyone does the same. If a vehicle mimics your action, it's time to move. If you're on a double-lane surface road, make a radical turn (such as a U-turn) to throw off your pursuer, then double back so you are theoretically traveling behind your tailers. Travel slowly and nonchalantly; you may have already lost them at the U-turn. Remember: If they followed you on the first turn, they may not have anticipated your second. If they mimicked both, you have now forced their hand. Whether you like it or not, you are now involved in an all-out chase.

4. PRACTICE VEHICULAR EVASION (ON FREEWAYS).

If you're being pursued on a freeway, scan the roadway for the nearest exit. Stay in the lane

112

111

110

109

108

107

106

105

104

103

102

101

100

099

098

097

096

095

094

093

092

091

090

089

088

087

086

085

084

farthest from the exit. Travel at or slightly above the posted speed limit. Wait for the exit to draw into sight. At the last possible second, cut over two, three, or four lanes—whatever is necessary—and exit the roadway. This is dangerous, and only you and your CTU instructors know if you are capable of pulling it off, but this tactic will lose 90 percent of all pursuers. Clever pursuers may still be onto you as soon as they can make it to the next exit and double back, but you can use your time advantage to lose yourself in local side streets, switch vehicles, or phone for back-up.

5. PRACTICE TECHNOLOGICAL EVASION.

Just because you can't see them doesn't mean they're not still there. If you cannot see the tail, but feel in your gut that you are being tracked—or have heard from the floor that you are— sweep for, eliminate, or disable all possible tracking devices.

Unfortunately, it is very difficult to eliminate tracking devices without adequate counter-measure technology. To complicate matters, trackers (or "bugs") may use one of several different technologies, such as optical devices (or lasers), electromagnetic devices (magnetic fields), acoustic devices (sound waves), and so on. Field agents can request one of our new electromagnetic detectors. They are about the size of a car door opener and fit conveniently on any keychain.

If you do not have one of these devices, an electromagnetic tracker can usually be found by using an agency walkie-talkie tuned to frequency 17, with its volume knob on the highest setting. This method was used on Day 5 by Audrey Raines when she was being followed by agents with Homeland Security. By transferring this device to another vehicle, she was able to evade her pursuers. Although her actions were not condoned by Homeland Security or CTU, the method she employed can be helpful in sanctioned situations.

Lacking either a walkie-talkie or a bona fide detector, you can slowly slide a magnetic compass across the suspected surface. When the compass enters the magnetic field, the needle will move. Unfortunately, this method—and the ones previously described—work only with electromagnetic trackers. If you do not have any tools, sweep for trackers by sight and feel; destroy the device or plant it on a moving decoy. Always keep in mind the following locations when sweeping for a tracking device:

- **On a vehicle:** the four wheel wells, the front and back bumpers, the underside of all four fenders, under or in the crack of car seats, and under the carpet. Most hostiles will not place trackers under a car's hood because excess heat can damage the device, and popping a hood may draw attention.
- **On your clothing or possessions:** the hem of any garment, shoe soles, jewelry, watches, and

113
112
111
110
109
108
107
106
105
104
103
102
101
100
099
098
097
096
095
094
093
092
091
090
089
088
087
086
085

pens. Remove the batteries from PDAs and mobile phones, which can be tracked by passive triangulation even when the power is switched off.

- **On your body:** the nape of the neck, subcutaneously. For proper removal of such a device—and a more extensive discussion of the four other most likely locations on your body—see the Health Clinic director.

If you cannot locate a device but feel strongly that it is there, abandon the vehicle. Stop driving and hide the vehicle in a secure location. Walk briskly to a new vehicle, break in, and hot-wire it to make your escape. If you are abandoning a CTU vehicle, please make careful note of its location and, at your earliest convenience, phone in its coordinates to the floor.

6. USE ADROIT MANEUVERS TO ESCAPE ALL-OUT CHASES.

Only dangerous or desperate criminals would continue to pursue an agent after that agent has expressed knowledge that he or she is being tailed. If they continue to follow you, consider this a definite threat. Phone CTU and await further instructions. If this is not possible, consider some of these extreme measures:

- Drive directly to CTU, a local police precinct, or some other law enforcement agency. The criminals will abandon their pursuit.
- Drive to a heavily populated location. Your speed and defensive driving will attract attention of civilians and local law enforcement. (Be aware that you are putting your fellow law enforcement brethren and civilians at risk.)
- Park your vehicle, use it as a shield, draw your weapon, and commence firing.
- Sacrifice yourself and your vehicle by driving off a precipice. This method, while the most extreme we have witnessed in our years at CTU, saved the life of Secretary Heller on Day 5, when his car was pursued by menacing associates of former CTU agent Christopher Henderson. To escape armed attackers tracking him via helicopter, Secretary Heller drove his vehicle off a cliff and into a lake. Before attempting this maneuver, agents should understand there are no predictable parameters that would ensure your survival, and no CTU-sanctioned training supports this technique. That Heller survived is a tribute to his stamina, excellent physical conditioning, and status as a fine and upstanding American.

GO WITH YOUR GUT. IF YOU
FEEL LIKE YOU'RE BEING
TAILED, YOU PROBABLY ARE.

| D | UNDERCOVER OPS |

SOME MISSIONS HAVE TO BE CONDUCTED BENEATH THE RADAR.
THESE MISSIONS, WHILE NECESSARY, ARE OFTEN TOO RISKY AND
INVOLVE TACTICS THAT ARE CONSIDERED TOO CONTROVERSIAL
TO BE MADE COMMON KNOWLEDGE TO ALL LEVELS AND MEMBERS
OF THE AGENCY. PROTOCOLS WILL BE IGNORED AND LIVES MAY BE
SACRIFICED IN ORDER TO SET THINGS IN MOTION. MOST IMPOR-
TANT, A LEVEL OF SECRECY IS ALSO NECESSARY TO PROTECT THE
INTEGRITY OF AN AGENT'S COVER.

117
116
115
114
113
112
111
110
109
108
107
106
105
104
103
102

All undercover ops must have the approval of the CTU director. However, be aware that securing a go for an undercover op from the director of CTU in no way shields you from reprimands from District, Division, and the White House. On Day 3, when District Director Ryan Chappelle learned of the sting operation that CTU director Tony Almeida and Agents Gael Ortega and Jack Bauer orchestrated so that Bauer could reestablish his cover with the Salazar crime organization, Chappelle's response was pointed: "You better find Bauer and make this thing work. Otherwise the two of you and Jack, assuming he's still alive, are gonna take the fall for everything that happened today, from the prison riots to Salazar's escape and every dead body in between." In short: If you establish an undercover op, even with the approval and participation of the CTU director, there are no guarantees that it will be a success and universally well received. Use your judgment.

Although "benign deception" is often a necessary part of a successful undercover op, it can still put a strain on office relationships and even threaten your career should things go awry. Most people do not appreciate being kept out of the loop, and their insecurities may get in the way of their seeing the bigger picture. Those agents who were not privy to the details of the operation may feel left out or fear they cannot be trusted. If you ever find yourself in this situation, it is important, as always, to keep your feelings and ego out of your work. Just keep in mind that if everyone knows about an undercover op, it won't remain undercover for long.

101
100
099
098
097
096
095
094
093
092
091
090
089

01 ESTABLISHING A FALSE IDENTITY

Undercover operations require intense advance work and painstaking attention to detail. Tough decisions are necessary, and sacrifices must be made. When Agent Bauer needed to reestablish his role within the Salazar crime organization to prevent the sale of a dangerous bioweapon by Ukrainian scientists, the setup required the jailbreak of a drug lord and cost many lives, among other things, to make the operation believable. It can take months to create a viable false identity. You are creating a whole person—someone with a history, friends, business associates, and habits. When months of planning are not possible, keep the following in mind as a quick reference.

118
117
116
115
114
113
112
111
110
109
108
107
106
105
104
103
102
101
100
099
098
097
096
095
094
093
092
091
090

PROFESSIONAL UNIFORMS MAKE FOR QUICK AND EFFECTIVE DISGUISES.

119
118
117
116
115
114
113
112
111
110
109
108
107
106
105
104
103
102
101
100
099
098
097
096
095
094
093
092
091

DO YOUR HOMEWORK.

It goes without saying—but we'll emphasize it here—that you must know every aspect of your false iden-tity. You must also know the organization you are infiltrating, inside and out. Strive to understand the subtleties of the way they work: what will impress them, what will enrage them, what is important to them, what they fear. Know their friends and their enemies, because you are, essentially, both.

COVER YOUR TRACKS.

Files. Information. Contacts. The web of proof you weave must be sturdy enough to support any level of scrutiny. You must have evidence in place that explains who you say you are now and what that person has done in the past. On Day 2, when Agent Bauer reestablished his cover as "Jack Roush" with the domestic antigovernment terrorist organization led by Joseph Wald, a full prison file from the state of Florida was created and uploaded onto the appropriate databases so that, should anyone check him out, the information he gave them would match up. Whenever possible, it's also desirable to include real people who can support your story, such as the police officer from Florida who was on call to verify that "Jack Roush" was out on parole.

DON'T APPEAR OVEREAGER.

Although you want to be sure to get "inside," don't overplay your hand. As with dating, making your-self too available can sometimes work to your disadvantage. Terrorists are secretive and will not respond well to someone who appears too eager.

CREATE TRUST.

Criminals are not trusting by nature. To gain their trust, you will need to give them something they want, make a dramatic gesture, or, ideally, both. To reestablish cover with the Salazars on Day 3, Agent Bauer broke Ramon Salazar out of prison. On Day 2, to gain the trust of Eddie Grant, second in charge to Joseph Wald, Bauer presented Grant with the severed head of Marshall Goren, key witness in a case against Wald. The life sacrificed—that of a known pedophile—was a necessary one for overall opera-tion success.

USE SMALLER TRUTHS TO SUPPORT THE LARGER LIE.

Speaking the truth conveys a believability that will enhance any falsehood. On Day 3, Agent Bauer was rejoining the Salazar crime organization, not establishing a new cover. Bauer had been responsible for Ramon Salazar's incarceration. The Salazars knew Bauer worked for CTU. Agent Bauer's ability to con-vince the Salazars that he should be trusted was rooted in his ability to use elements of the truth to create a more believable lie. "I'm done putting my ass on the line for nothing," Bauer convincingly said to Hector and Ramon Salazar. Agent Bauer then added emotionally charged information about the

TO REESTABLISH COVER WITH THE SALAZARS
ON DAY 3, AGENT JACK BAUER BROKE
RAMON SALAZAR OUT OF PRISON.

118
117
116
115
114
113
112
111
110
109
108
107
106
105
104
103
102
101
100
099
098
097
096
095
094
093
092

121
120
119
118
117
116
115
114
113
112
111
110
109
108
107
106
105
104
103
102
101
100
099
098
097
096
095
094
093

death of his wife, Teri, about his daughter hating him, and about his heroin addiction—all of which were, at one time or another, true. Bauer used these very real and emotionally charged facts to embellish his overall comments about his dissatisfaction with CTU and desire to leave behind his life as an agent. Bauer used real suffering in his life to convince them of a lie. The pain and frustration behind his statements made him believable.

DISPEL SUSPICION.

When establishing cover, some people are easier to convince than others. It is up to you to read the situation quickly and correctly and to identify the person or persons likely to cause you the most trouble. Once that has been accomplished, shift suspicion away from you and toward those individuals. On Day 2, Agent Bauer knew that "Dave" stood to thwart his successful reentry into Wald's organization. Bauer's vehement criticism of Dave's abilities—that he tied his explosive fuses too tightly—not only put Dave on the defensive but also caused him to jump Bauer, giving Bauer the opportunity to put him out of commission by breaking his ankle. Although you do not always want to attract unnecessary attention, a certain degree of alpha-dog behavior can go a long way under the right circumstances.

OFFER THEM SOMETHING THEY WANT.

Terrorists want what most people want: Money. Power. Influence. Revenge. On Day 3, the carrot that Agent Bauer dangled in front of the Salazar brothers was the brokering of a deal for a bioweapon that would net them nearly one billion dollars in profit. Greed usually overrides logic.

IMPORTANT

Turn off your cell phone or set it to vibrate. A call from family or friends at an inopportune time can cost you not only your cover but, possibly, your life.

122
121
120
119
118
117
116
115
114
113
112
111
110
109
108
107
106
105
104
103
102
101
100
099
098
097
096
095
094

A NOTE ABOUT YOUR MENTAL HEALTH

Going undercover can take a great toll on your emotional health, especially over long periods. We cannot stress enough that having a good handle on who you are before you go undercover will help you maintain a healthy identity during and after your mission. For the weak-willed, it's easy to get lost in—or even seduced by—that world.

Going undercover is like method acting: You can never be out of character, yet you must remember that you are playing a character. The most obvious difference between acting and going undercover is that, when a method actor has a bad day, he or she gets a bad review. When an undercover operative has a bad day, he or she can end up dead, jeopardizing a mission and costing innocent lives.

02 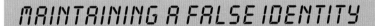 MAINTAINING A FALSE IDENTITY

Make no mistake about deep cover—you will be constantly tested. Very few agents possess the mental, physical, and emotional constitution to maintain a cover successfully and for long periods. While there may be no "I" in "team," there is without a doubt no "we" in "undercover." When you go undercover, understand that CTU will provide any support that the situation allows. But you are, at the end of the day, utterly alone. Despite this state of affairs, you still need to be sure to convey information back to CTU in any way possible. You have not gone dark, and you are expected to do your best to relay your position and any intel back to the agent running point for you on the floor.

PROVE YOUR LOYALTY.

Moments will arise—no matter how long you have maintained your cover—when you will be asked to further prove that you are, in fact, who you say you are. You can choose to create these opportunities to boost your reputation with the organization you have infiltrated, or you may have these challenges foisted upon you. In either case, your ability to be convincing, no matter the situation, is what counts.

123
122
121
120
119
118
117
116
115
114
113
112
111
110
109
108
107
106
105
104
103
102
101
100
099
098
097
096
095

CREATING EMOTIONAL BONDS WHILE UNDERCOVER MAY EXPEDITE THE RELEASE OF INFORMATION.

This ability is best exhibited by Agent Bauer's behavior on Day 3. Bauer was asked by Hector Salazar to shoot the captured CTU agent Chase Edmunds. "You keep saying you are on our side. Now prove it—once and for all." Agent Bauer did what was required to maintain his cover and cement the trust of Salazar. Luckily for Bauer and Edmunds, the gun was not loaded. The situation could have very well turned out otherwise, but Agent Bauer made the right choice for the overall success of the mission.

EMBRACE THE LIFESTYLE.

To use the parlance of our times, "go with the flow." That can involve as little as a change in sleeping habits and clothing. However, extenuating circumstances may require you to commit felonies or even use heavy narcotics. (For guidelines on illegal drug use while undercover, see section D3, page 96.) All you can do is use your best judgment when trying to strike a balance between maintaining your cover and engaging in illegal activity.

124
123
122
121
120
119
118
117
116
115
114
113
112
111
110
109
108
107
106
105
104
103
102
101
100
099
098
097
096

STAY FOCUSED ON THE BIG PICTURE.

While undercover, it is often necessary to look the other way in the face of very difficult circumstances. In addition to allowing crimes to be committed right in front of you, you may also need to actively participate. On Day 2, Agent Bauer, undercover as "Jack Roush," helped orchestrate the bombing of CTU. In doing so, he gleaned valuable information that helped stop a nuclear threat. Staying focused on the mission objectives may be the only thing that keeps you going when faced with unspeakable crimes and the deaths of innocent victims.

MANIPULATE RELATIONSHIPS.

This includes creating opportunities to bond emotionally with key individuals who may give you valuable information and exposing the frailties in other key relationships. Agent Bauer exploited the existing tension and competition between Ramon and Hector Salazar to draw attention away from himself, and he also developed a romantic relationship with Hector Salazar's significant other, Claudia. Bauer's relationship with Claudia made it possible for him to contact CTU while undercover. Be aware: Lines can become blurred, and anyone who becomes involved with you will be in danger.

GERMAN INTELLIGENCE AGENT THEO STOLLER WENT UNDERCOVER TO OBTAIN INFORMATION FROM COLLETTE STEGNER.

125
124
123
122
121
120
119
118
117
116
115
114
113
112
111
110
109
108
107
106
105
104
103
102
101
100
099
098
097
96

KNOW WHEN YOU'RE IN OVER YOUR HEAD.

An agent operating undercover can end up in a situation where both the mission objective and the life of that agent are in danger. If an undercover situation becomes untenable, contact CTU, if possible. Arrangements for safe extraction will be activated.

03   *ILLEGAL DRUG USE: HOW TO AVOID IT*

Illegal drugs are a fact of life in the underworld investigated by CTU. Narcotics are often the quickest way for a terrorist organization to raise funds, and the narcotics supply chain provides a logical nexus for underworld figures to enlarge their interpersonal connections, recruit personnel, and acquire weapons and other technology. If you are forced to interact with this world during an investigation, you must be prepared to deal with, and be exposed to, narcotics.

CTU's policy on record is strict on this matter. We do not tolerate illegal drug use. Any agent found to be using drugs on the premises will be immediately punished and possibly arrested. Drug use in your personal life or "off-time," whether induced by job-related stress or otherwise, is grounds for investigation, suspension, reassignment to another agency, and/or dismissal.

That being said, CTU recognizes its responsibility to agents who may have been exposed to narcotics in the course of an undercover investigation. Should CTU become aware of an agent's drug use—no matter what the circumstance—we will work to arrange counseling, psychiatric evaluation, and a fair and considerate review of that agent's case. Leniency in these instances is possible, but should neither be expected by the agent nor promised by his or her superiors. Reports of investigations and reviews will be routed through the entire chain of command, up to District. All reports—and the final decision—will become part of the agent's permanent dossier.

The events of Day 3 helped shape this policy. Drawing on what the agency learned in the course of the day and the debriefings that followed, we offer the following as a guide to undercover agents who may encounter drugs or be pressured to use drugs in the field to maintain their cover. Since you are usually working alone in undercover situations, only you will know when drug use is necessary to advance your mission—or if other needs are driving you.

UNDERSTAND THE LAW.

Regardless of your standing as a CTU agent, you are still breaking U.S. law if you use drugs while undercover. If your actions become public knowledge via the media, the agency must publicly condemn them and initiate an investigation.

DETERMINE THE NECESSITY OF DRUG USE.

Don't automatically assume you must resort to drug use. While it is not unheard of for the target of an investigation—a drug lord, terrorist leader, etc.—to pressure an undercover agent to do drugs as a "test," or a means of proving that he or she is not an undercover agent, we have learned that such "tests" are rare. (Drug lords typically eschew drug use themselves.) Ideally, you will embed yourself in the target's organization in such a way that your credibility is established in a manner that has nothing to do with drug use. (See D1, "Establishing a False Identity," page 88.) Regrettably, agents who use drugs while undercover are often acting on the misguided belief that they need to appear credible in their role. On Day 3, drug lord Ramon Salazar taunted Agent Bauer by saying: "When you were down there with us, I had no idea you were an agent. We accepted you. You didn't have to put the needle in your arm. You did that for other reasons. The same reason as all junkies. To kill the pain. What's your pain, Jack? What does the needle make go away?"

EVADE WITH MUNDANE RESPONSES.

A crime boss's underlings, however, may pressure you to indulge in drug use out of suspicion or jealousy, or as a gesture of friendship or generosity. Evade a request to do drugs with a boring response that does not call attention to itself. "I have a cold," "I'm busy right now," "I'm leaving in five minutes," and "I gotta stay focused for tonight" are all acceptable excuses. They imply that you have nothing against the behavior, just the timing of it. If someone challenges you, reframe the situation in such a way that you put the challenger on notice. Wherever possible, refer to the authority figure who is absent

126
125
124
123
122
121
120
119
118
117
116
115
114
113
112
111
110
109
108
107
106
105
104
103
102
101
100
099
098

127
126
125
124
123
122
121
120
119
118
117
116
115
114
113
112
111
110
109
108
107
106
105
104
103
102
101
100
099

and who may inspire fear in your challenger: "Are you crazy? Salazar would kill me if I got high before this job!"

IN DAY 3, JACK DEVELOPED A DRUG DEPENDENCY THAT ALMOST ENDED HIS CAREER.

GO LAST, AND FAKE IT.

If you simply cannot avoid using drugs, try to do so after everyone present has already done so. Their recollections of the moment will be clouded, and you may be able to get away with taking a lesser dose or faking it entirely. Health Clinic instructors can demonstrate how to administer a fake injection, effect "false swallow" of a pill, or achieve noninsufflation of a powdered substance.

USE A LESS PHYSICALLY ADDICTIVE DRUG.

If you cannot back out, and you are being closely watched, try to use a drug or drug variant that is not powerfully addictive. Not all drugs are created equal. Heroin is the most rapidly acting of all known opi-

128
127
126
125
124
123
122
121
120
119
118
117
116
115
114
113
112
111
110
109
108
107
106
105
104
103
102
101
100

ates, so Agent Bauer's situation may have been ameliorated had he chosen cocaine instead. CTU realizes you may not always have this choice.

CONTROL IT.

Once you have used a narcotic, you must assess whether or not you can continue your mission. In most cases, it is still possible to do so. In the case of a highly addictive drug, you may be compelled to continue usage. Resist, using all the strategies previously discussed. If you must, use sparingly and cease use as soon as your mission is completed. Report all usage to your SAC or supervisor as soon as possible. Addiction can be chemically treated, but we understand that this is often impractical while you are on assignment. Nevertheless, you are bound by CTU's drug use statement—which you signed when you entered the agency—to disclose any and all use of narcotics during undercover operations.

I M P O R T A N T

Under no circumstances are you to withhold information about your drug use from your superiors or fellow agents for fear of further CTU action. Your continued use of the drug, or difficulty kicking the habit, can put your health, your job, and the lives of your colleagues on the line. On Day 3, Agent Bauer openly declared to Agent Edmunds, "I'm not going on record with this addiction." This admission placed Edmunds in a position where he felt compelled to cover for his partner, and their mission may have been jeopardized. Always disclose. It is the only way we can get you the treatment you need.

129
128
127
126
125
124
123
122
121
120
119
118
117
116
115
114
113
112
111
110
109
108
107
106
105
104
103
102
101

04 — HOW TO "GO DARK"

In recent CTU history, agents have felt compelled to go dark so that they could better perform their missions. Whether this strategy is effective is an ongoing debate in the intelligence-gathering community. Though the strategy may have its uses, it can backfire, jeopardizing agents as well as their colleagues, friends, family, and CTU missions. The tactic should be undertaken only as a last resort. What follows is a discussion of the method and a brief synopsis of agency response and policy.

DEFINITION

When a CTU agent goes dark, he or she ceases any and all communication with the floor, fellow agents in the field, and even personal friends and family members. The agent remains incommunicado until such time as he or she feels the mission has sufficiently progressed—either successfully or unsuccessfully—to permit a return to CTU and private life. This period of noncommunication may last hours, days, months, or possibly longer. The stratagem and its terminology do not originate with CTU. Military Special Forces have been known to go dark to conduct highly sensitive operations that a civilian command is likely to rescind in the eleventh hour. Private corporations have been said to go dark when they withhold highly sensitive information from their boards or shareholders.

METHODOLOGY AND CAVEATS

Going dark is remarkably simple in theory and requires that one cease all communication with CTU and known associates. In some cases, agents have disposed of their phones and all tracking devices that could pinpoint their location. If the dark period endures a long time, the agent may also cease all contact with friends and family, dispose of or securely cache all personal documents, assume a new identity, and access a secret stash of funds. When a "dark" agent needs to communicate with a trusted confidant, he or she uses face-to-face meetings or phones equipped with subchannel chips, which are designed to receive a specific signal and cannot be traced. Scramble filters may also be used, allowing one to speak unfiltered on a regular cell phone for up to one minute. (A cheap, disposable prepaid cell phone is usually the instrument of choice.) Needless to say, long-term dark periods are extremely difficult to accomplish unless one has extensive personal and financial resources.

UPON GOING DARK, AN AGENT
SEVERS ALL CONTACT WITH
CTU EMPLOYEES AND
RESOURCES. IT IS TRULY AN
OPTION OF LAST RESORT.

130
129
128
127
126
125
124
123
122
121
120
119
118
117
116
115
114
113
112
111
110
109
108
107
106
105
104
103
102
101

131
130
129
128
127
126
125
124
123
122
121
120
119
118
117
116
115
114
113
112
111
110
109
108
107
106
105
104
103

In extreme cases, an individual who has gone dark may be presumed dead and may be forced to take up menial, cash-only work to cover living expenses. (For recent history and discussion, see D5, "How to Fake Your Own Death," page 103.)

JUSTIFIABLE REASONS A CTU AGENT MIGHT GO DARK:

- The United States has undergone a hostile takeover by a terrorist organization or enemy power, and the agent has reason to believe his or her orders are working counter to the best interests of the citizens of the United States.
- The CTU chain of command has been corrupted by dangerously incompetent management, and the agent cannot, in good conscience, continue to accept orders from those in charge.
- One or more CTU agents (working the floor or in the field) are believed to be moles or undercover operatives for hostile organizations, and the agent cannot ascertain the integrity of any CTU agents with whom he or she speaks.

UNJUSTIFIABLE REASONS A CTU AGENT MIGHT GO DARK:

- The agent does not agree with stated orders or anticipated orders from CTU supervisors.
- The agent possesses highly revealing, explosive, or sensitive intel that no one else has but does not see fit to share it with colleagues or superiors.
- The agent has decided that he or she knows best and will do better operating alone.

As you can see, a fine line separates both sets of reasons. An agent may be operating under erroneous assumptions brought on by stress and may not be in the best condition to judge whether an action is justifiable or unjustifiable. A personal conflict with a superior might lead an agent to believe that the superior is "dangerously incompetent"; but nine out of ten fellow agents would disagree with your assessment. It is often a matter of judgment, and judgments can be wrong. In a 1997 paper presented at an intelligence-gathering conference at Langley, two authors researched, reviewed, and analyzed eighteen "go-dark" cases from CTU, CIA, NSA, and DOD history and found that only one was justifiable. Since that seminal presentation—by Agents Richard Walsh and Christopher Henderson—agency policy has been highly skeptical of agents' decisions to go dark. Currently, all go-dark cases are to be reviewed at the district level, and the agents involved are subject to debriefings and sanctions by the inspector general's office.

Case in point: On Day 3, Agent Edmunds disobeyed Agent Bauer's orders to return to CTU from the field. Believing that Bauer had been captured and transported against his will to Mexico by the Salazar narcotics organization, Edmunds opted to go dark and pursue several leads without briefing his supervisors or notifying the floor. He crossed the border to Mexico and was captured and tortured by the Salazars' men. Though Edmunds believed he was correct to do all in his power to rescue his partner, he

132
131
130
129
128
127
126
125
124
123
122
121
120
119
118
117
116
115
114
113
112
111
110
109
108
107
106
105
104

:hat Bauer had willingly undertaken a sensitive undercover operation. By ceasing all com-
th CTU, Edmunds put himself and his fellow agent in greater danger. Let that be a les-
rk cuts you off from your most precious resource and our stock-in-trade—intel. If you
lark, you are on your own. Consider it carefully.

HOW TO FAKE YOUR OWN DEATH

Unnecessary loss of life is something that we obviously strive to avoid at CTU, for our agents and for the citizens we protect. Extenuating circumstances may arise when an agent is faced with only one option for survival—to fake death. There is no official "order" to fake a death, and CTU cannot approve or sanction an agent's decision to do so. However, in CTU history, agents have found themselves with no other viable or realistic alternative. The most notable example occurred on Day 4 when Agent Bauer faked his death, which seemed the only alternative to avoid incarceration and torture in a Chinese prison. Unfortunately, Bauer was able to conceal his identity for only eighteen months, after which time he ended up in exactly the place he was trying to avoid—a Chinese prison. You must understand that the ramifications, legal or otherwise, resulting from a decision to fake your own death will be borne by you alone. Therefore, it is not advisable to take a decision of this sort lightly. Should it be absolutely necessary, however, several methods have proved to be effective.

NS AND FIRES

›n caused by explosions and fires is the perfect way to hide evidence, including human
a sizable explosion, it is possible that no search will be undertaken to identify victims.
‹ne someone can sift through the debris and retrieve dental records or other incontrovert-

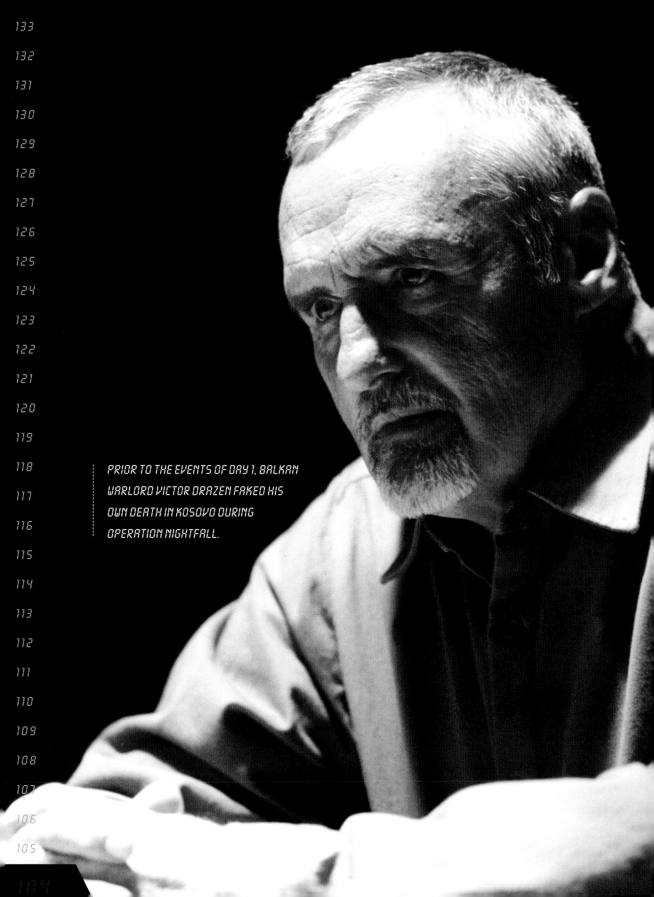

133

132

131

130

129

128

127

126

125

124

123

122

121

120

119

118

117

116

115

114

113

112

111

110

109

108

107

106

105

104

PRIOR TO THE EVENTS OF DAY 1, BALKAN WARLORD VICTOR DRAZEN FAKED HIS OWN DEATH IN KOSOVO DURING OPERATION NIGHTFALL.

134
133
132
131
130
129
128
127
126
125
124
123
122
121
120
119
118
117
116
115
114
113
112
111
110
109
108
107
106

ible evidence, an agent would have plenty of time to move on from the scene. Victor Drazen accomplished this ruse with great success during Operation Nightfall: He was believed to be dead until he resurfaced on Day 1 to orchestrate an attempted assassination of senator and presidential candidate David Palmer and Agent Jack Bauer. The explosion in Kosovo was so powerful that no one thought to look for his remains.

DROWNING

Faking a drowning requires excellent skills as a swimmer and, more often than not, a bit of luck. The ability to stay underwater and avoid being sighted is necessary, although it is hard to determine just how diligent the pursuing hostiles will be in seeking to verify your status. This strategy works best in seas or oceans since there is no way to drag the body of water for proof.

INJECTION OR INGESTION

A trickier proposition for faking death—but one that can be virtually foolproof—is to inject or ingest a class of beta-blockers that will slow down the pulse to the point where the person will appear to be dead. Metoprolol and atenolol, for example, are commonly available beta-blockers used to treat arrhythmias and other cardiac diseases that may slow the pulse enough to create the desired effect. Riskier is tetrodotoxin, a neurotoxin derived from puffer fish that is rumored to be a favorite of voodoo practitioners; it can give the subject the appearance of being near death or in a zombie-like state for days. If any of these approaches is used, it may result in actual death. This very real danger must be taken into account. You will need to enlist an accomplice to bring the individual's vitals back to a healthy state by administering epinephrine to the heart, followed by CPR. Again: This method should be considered only as a last resort.

TRUSTING OTHERS WITH YOUR SECRET

If you opt to stage your death, you will likely need to enlist the help of trusted friends or colleagues. You should involve only those individuals who absolutely need to know, for their safety as much as yours. When Agent Bauer faked his death, only former president David Palmer and Agents Dessler, Almeida, and O'Brian knew of his plan. Considering that three of those individuals lost their lives as a result of the information they possessed, it is possible that four people in the know is three too many.

UNINTENTIONALLY FAKING YOUR DEATH

Situations may arise in the line of duty where you will be presumed dead through no plan of your own. Although alarming to colleagues and loved ones, this circumstance can also work to your advantage. Attention is shifted away from you, and no one will see you coming. It is akin to going permanently dark. Individuals have for years used this sort of error to their advantage, such as Stephen Saunders, a for-

131
130
129
128
127
126
125
124
123
122
121
120
119
118
117
116
115
114
113
112
111
110
109
108
107
106

IF YOU USE A BETA-BLOCKING INJEC-
TION TO FAKE YOUR OWN DEATH, BE
CERTAIN ANOTHER AGENT IS READY
TO REVIVE YOU.

mer British intelligence agent who took part in Operation Nightfall in Kosovo, which targeted the Drazen family. Saunders was believed killed during that mission. His newfound anonymity allowed him to operate under the radar for years, and he resurfaced only to unleash the deadly Cordilla virus in Los Angeles. On Day 5, when Omicron executive and former CTU director Christopher Henderson believed Agent Bauer was killed in an explosion he staged, the last place he expected Bauer to show up was at his home—but that's exactly what happened.

I M P O R T A N T

Just as you may be wrongly presumed dead, it is also possible that you may wrongly presume a terrorist is dead. The terrorist would benefit from the same advantages outlined in the preceding pages. Before you write off a threat to national security, you must be absolutely certain of the status of persons of interest believed to have been killed in an explosion.

136
135
134
133
132
131
130
129
128
127
126

IF DEATH IS (REALLY) THE ONLY OPTION

An unfortunate reality for career counterterrorism agents is that capture is always a possibility. And it follows that capture may very well result in torture. Information is our most valuable currency, and keeping it safe is our top priority at CTU. Though self-induced death is not an action we like to encourage, suicide capsules are available for field agents in the event they are captured. Ingesting these will prevent torture and the release of valuable information. The tablets will make you feel as if you're going to sleep. Under *no* circumstances are these capsules to be made available to civilians. This protocol was disregarded on Day 3 when guests at the Chandler Plaza Hotel in Los Angeles were infected with the Cordilla virus, and Agent Dessler was adamant about making this option available to them. When former regional director Ryan Chappelle was approached by Agent Almeida to obtain permission to distribute the capsules, Chappelle simply said, "It's against every regulation in the book . . . Do it." CTU did not condone the use of suicide capsules in what essentially amounted to a government-sanctioned mass suicide. Had Chappelle not been killed in the line of duty later that day, he would have been subject to severe reprimands.

AGENT JACK BAUER USED AN EXPLOSION—
AND THE ELEMENT OF SURPRISE—
TO GREAT EFFECT ON DAY 5.

125
124
123
122
121
120
119
118
117
116
115
114
113
112
111
110
109
108
107

137
136
135
134
133
132
131
130
129
128
127
126
125
124
123
122
121
120
119
118
117
116
115
114
113
112
111
110
109

STARTING OVER: NOTES ON A NEW LIFE

Once a faked death has been successfully achieved, it will usually be necessary for the agent to resurface and reenter the world under a new identity. Doing so is similar to going undercover, but there are some key differences. While undercover, you know that there is an end to the mission, a purpose to your actions. When assuming a completely new identity, there is no vacation, no time off, no end in sight. The differences between going undercover and living a new life are largely psychological, but they are nonetheless significant, and they can have a profound effect on individuals seeking to adjust to their new way of life. The permanence of a new identity can be hard to handle. In fact, some agents choose to change identities constantly, opting to stay on the move, changing passports and addresses on a regular basis. The more stable option, however, is to start fresh and forge one new identity for as long as you can safely maintain it. After faking his death on Day 4, Agent Jack Bauer lived as "Frank Flynn" to save his own life and protect his daughter.

There is no one way to lead life under a new identity, but here are some guidelines to keep in mind.

KEEP A LOW PROFILE.

While living your new life, avoid attracting attention. Your identity is false, so you should not leave a paper trail bearing your new name. Try not to sign documents or get any bills in your assumed name. Rent a room in someone's house rather than signing a lease. Get work that pays in cash—such as construction, restaurant work, or landscaping—rather than filling out an application or filing a W-9.

BE MISERLY WITH YOUR INFORMATION.

The people you will get to know in your new life will be as interested as anyone else about who you are and where you came from. Give them just enough information to satisfy their curiosity, but not so much that it arouses more suspicion. It is especially important not to give information that can be easily confirmed or disproved. "I was working construction in Portland . . . I moved from job to job . . . I was living out of my car at the time . . . " If someone asks you if you knew so-and-so while you were living in Portland, it's generally best to say "no." It's easier to explain how or why you don't know someone than it is to explain how you do know someone who says they don't know you.

MONITOR YOUR EMOTIONAL INVOLVEMENT.

As tempting as it is to begin again in all areas of your life—including your personal relationships—it's best to avoid becoming attached, for your safety as well as for the well-being of those with whom you are beginning to bond. Agent Bauer's inability to remain detached while living with Diane Huxley and her son Derek in California left more emotional wreckage in the wake of his blown cover than was necessary, and it put Derek's life at risk as well.

AGENT JACK BAUER LIVED WITH DIANE HUXLEY AND HER SON DEREK DURING HIS SHORT LIFE AS "FRANK FLYNN."

138
137
136
135
134
133
132
131
130
129
128
127
126
125
124
123
122
121
120
119
118
117
116
115
114
113
112
111
110

DESTROY THIS HANDBOOK.

If anyone discovers this book among your belongings, you will have a difficult time explaining how you came to own a top-secret government handbook. Use fire to reduce the pages to ashes. Should you ever return to your old life as a CTU agent, your supervisor will supply a new copy of the handbook.

E COMBAT

CTU RELIES HEAVILY ON UP-TO-DATE INTELLIGENCE, SEEKS TO
STOP TERRORISTS BEFORE THEY GET STARTED, AND AIMS TO
SOLVE PROBLEMS WITH MINIMAL PAIN, SUFFERING, AND LOSS OF
LIFE. NEVERTHELESS, COMBAT IS AN UNAVOIDABLE PART OF
YOUR LIFE AS AN AGENT. COMBAT IS SOMETHING WE TRAIN FOR
AND SOMETHING WE EXCEL AT. TRAINING AT CTU IS INTENSE AND
VARIED AND IS DESIGNED TO COVER AS MANY CONTINGENCIES AS
POSSIBLE. WHILE MUCH OF THE TRAINING THAT WE FOCUS ON
INVOLVES HAND-TO-HAND COMBAT, PHYSICAL CONDITIONING, AND
WEAPONS TRAINING, YOUR MENTAL EDGE AND ATTITUDE UNDER
PRESSURE ARE INVALUABLE ASSETS TO ANY AND EVERY MIS-
SION. CTU'S GREATEST ADVANTAGE DURING COMBAT, THE MOST
POWERFUL WEAPON WE WIELD, IS THE COMBINED STRENGTH OF
OUR AGENTS' MINDS AND MORAL RESOLVE.

141
140
139
138
137
136
135
134
133
132
131
130
129
128
127
126
125
124
123
122
121
120
119
118
117
116
115
114
113

FIELD AGENT HAND SIGNALS

During field operations, camouflaging your position and your presence is one of the keys to maintaining the element of surprise, which may mean the difference between a successful mission and a tragic failure. Hand signals are routinely used by special ops units of the armed forces, federal agencies, SWAT teams, and other organizations to help them move as a unit and coordinate their actions while under the cover of silence.

Variant signals depend on the mission and the lead organization in the field. The following are standard field agent hand signals for CTU field operations.

YOU	ME	COME	COVER THIS AREA	GO HERE OR MOVE
HURRY UP	STOP	FREEZE	LISTEN OR I HEAR	WATCH OR I SEE
ENEMY	HOSTAGE	DOG	SNIPER	CELL LEADER
I DON'T UNDERSTAND	I UNDERSTAND	CROUCH OR GO PRONE	GAS	BREACH(ER)

142
141
140
139
138
137
136
135
134
133
132
131
130
129
128
127
126
125
124
123
122
121
120
119
118
117
116
115
114

SECURING THE PERIMETER

Intelligence and field agents often need to set up security perimeters in conjunction with CTU Tactical. By definition, a perimeter is a well-coordinated cordon of heavily armed agents and Tac team members who isolate and confine a precise geographical location for the purposes of carrying out a specific mission. Typically, security perimeters are established for one or more of the following reasons:

- A hostage situation

- A bomb, chemical, or bioterrorism threat

- A riot location

- A barricaded-hostile or hostile-in-flight crisis

- A special VIP or major public event

In practice, CTU usually establishes the following types of perimeters: soft and hard.

SOFT PERIMETER

Only civilians with a legitimate or compelling reason are permitted inside the outer or inner perimeters. That includes civilians with proof of nearby residence and local business owners and employees. Soft perimeters may sometimes need to be "silent"—that is, operating in such a way that both the civilians and hostiles in the perimeter zone will not be alerted to our presence.

HARD PERIMETER

The perimeter is strictly limited to CTU personnel and cooperating agency personnel. Civilians, if present, are either screened out or warned to take cover. Use of a hard perimeter usually indicates a crisis situation in progress. Regardless of the type of perimeter, CTU agents and Tac will be expected to:

- Monitor vehicular traffic
- Monitor flow of pedestrians
- Follow protocols for personnel safety and medical evacuation
- Establish and maintain contact with the CTU floor

143
142
141
140
139
138
137
136
135
134
133
132
131
130
129
128
127
126
125
124
123
122
121
120
119
118
117
116
115

STEPS TO ESTABLISHING A PERIMETER

1. START WITH THE INNER PERIMETER.

Confine the hostiles or the VIPs and legitimate friendly civilians to the smallest area possible, ideally inside a building. Dispatch assault teams to their positions and CTU sharpshooters to the nearest rooftops. Identify all entrances, windows, subterranean areas, and possible escape routes from adjoining rooftops within this area. Lock them down. Request satellite surveillance, if available. Upload any and all schematics of relevant structures to the PDAs of CTU team leaders.

2. ESTABLISH THE OUTER PERIMETER.

Keep out anyone not working on the mission or event. Determine the extent or radius of the perimeter and identify and establish screening points on all surrounding streets. Determine the need for barricades or support vehicles and place them where they will present a physical barrier to the cordoned area. For example, you may need a screening point for every main road within a six-block radius. Depending on the protocols of the mission, any pedestrian or vehicle approaching the area will be screened, challenged, or warned away entirely. In the case of special events, the outer perimeter must be wide enough to protect VIPs located in the inner perimeter from a conventional bomb detonation on the outer perimeter.

3. EVACUATE CIVILIANS TO THE OUTER PERIMETER.

Our goal is always to protect and spare innocent civilian life. But that is not always our mission. Know the difference. CTU operations happen quickly. In urban combat situations, you will not be able to evacuate all buildings, but you can keep pedestrians off the streets. Warn local residents to either stay in their homes or move outside the outer perimeter. Except in the most desolate areas of Los Angeles, you will need to divert traffic and employ crowd control measures.

4. ESTABLISH A COMMAND POST.

This site will be your staging area. It should be close to the inner perimeter but outside the expected line of fire. Establish all necessary COM links to CTU and any other cooperating agencies. Make sure everyone is on the same "page"—and frequency.

144

143

142

141

140

139

138

137

136

135

134

133

132

131

130

129

128

127

126

125

124

123

122

121

120

119

118

117

116

5. ESTABLISH A MEDICAL AREA.

Medics are typically stationed just inside the outer perimeter on a main road so that wounded personnel can be treated and evacuated immediately to a hospital or to the CTU Health Clinic. In the event of a bomb or bio or chemical threat, Hazmat respondents and their vehicles will be afforded an area close to the command post.

> WHEN SECURING THE PERIMETER, TRY TO CONFINE HOSTILES TO THE SMALLEST POSSIBLE AREAS.

6. ESTABLISH DEGREE-OF-FORCE PARAMETERS.

How will you treat civilians and hostiles who attempt to exit or penetrate the perimeter? This is an important one, so do not delay choosing parameters and disseminating this information to all involved agents and Tac team leaders. This order will come from your SAC or the highest-ranking CTU agent present on the floor. If at all possible, this decision should be made and the proper protocol put in place before the perimeters are set. This is not a decision that should

145
144
143
142
141
140
139
138
137
136
135
134
133
132
131
130
129
128
127
126

125
124
123
122
121
120
119
118
117

be made in the course of hostile engagement or other crisis. In the case of the Chandler Plaza Hotel incident on Day 3, a shoot-to-kill parameter was enforced to prevent the spread of the Cordilla virus.

> USING EXPLOSIVE DEVICES TO BREACH A PERIMETER WILL FOSTER AN ELEMENT OF SURPRISE.

TIPS FOR SETTING UP A PERIMETER

- **Time is always of the essence.** CTU Tactical has a superior record for perimeter setup. But if Tac cannot get the job done in time, field agents must be prepared to enter an insecure location without backup. Do so only with your SAC's authorization.

148

145

144

143

142

141

140

139

138

137

136

135

134

133

132

131

130

129

128

127

126

125

124

123

122

121

120

119

118

- **Don't be overly ambitious.** The size of your perimeter should be determined by the number of personnel at your disposal. The larger the perimeter, the more eyes, bodies, and guns you will need to cover the territory.

- **Coordinate with local law enforcement whenever possible.** It is virtually impossible to set up a hard or soft perimeter without alerting some civilians to your presence. Eventually, someone will notify local law enforcement, and if local police hears about an operation from a civilian before they hear about it from CTU, someone will need to be debriefed later. We know it is not always possible or wise to alert the police to an operation, but in most cases it should be done as a courtesy. We will need their help—especially if the op impacts a large segment of the populace or residential community. It's also wise policy to strengthen interagency relations.

- **Familiarize yourself with security perimeter technology.** Some public areas in Los Angeles are fitted with retractable bollards that drop into the ground when an authorized vehicle approaches, then rise when the vehicle has passed. To ensure that your vehicle is welcomed, make sure it is carrying an authorized transponder device that lowers the bollards. In the event of a power failure, the bollards can be lowered manually. All Tac team leaders and field agents must know how to operate the fail-safes on these devices so that you can get your vehicles close to certain high-security public buildings. Under no circumstances should you attempt to ram your vehicle through a line of bollards. The best of these are capable of stopping a 15,000-pound truck traveling at 50 miles per hour. You will damage your CTU vehicle, and it will be recorded in your permanent dossier.

147
146
145
144
143
142
141
140
139
138
137
136
135
134
133
132
131
130
129
128
127
126
125
124
123
122
121
120
119

F3 HAND-TO-HAND COMBAT

All field agents assigned to CTU have to demonstrate hand-to-hand combat proficiency in at least two disciplines. There are a variety of hand-to-hand combat approaches available, and many agents have trained elsewhere—with SWAT, Special Forces, or martial arts masters. A good deal of CTU's hand-to-hand training is rooted in Krav Maga, the official self-defense method of the Israeli defense forces, which is very popular among law enforcement agencies throughout the United States. The late Tony Almeida, former CTU director, was a certified Krav Maga instructor and helped to establish an on-site Krav Maga training and certification program at CTU. If you wish to augment your current skills or become certified, inquire at the fitness center.

Your continued training—both physical and technical—is mandatory during your tenure at CTU. Below are general combat strategies and approaches.

KNOW YOUR OPPONENTS.

Do not underestimate them. Confidence in combat is a strength, but egotism that blinds you to the abilities and potential advantages of your opponents is a weakness.

WHEN POSSIBLE, USE WEAKNESSES AS STRENGTHS.

Not everything that initially appears to be a weakness is necessarily a weakness. For example, if you're significantly smaller than your opponent, remember that you have a lower center of gravity and can move more quickly. If your opponent has a gun and you have a knife, remember that your opponent will eventually need to reload and may run out of ammunition. Also keep in mind that the hostile may underestimate you—if you're lucky. In short, always maintain your mental edge.

STRIKE FIRST.

This statement may sound trite, but getting in the first strike can often give you the advantage, especially if that strike is well placed and directed at a pressure point. The element of surprise and the ability to hamper your opponent from the outset is always an advantage.

148
147
146
145
144
143
142
141
140
139
138

BLOCKING IS SOMETIMES BETTER THAN EVADING.

Many times, lunging back or to the side to avoid a first strike will place you off balance. Once you are off balance, you are markedly more vulnerable to a second strike from your attacker, who undoubtedly knows this and will take advantage of it. Whether the strike is aimed at the lower or upper half of your body, a basic block will keep you protected without sacrificing your footing. It also lets your attackers know that you can take whatever they can dish out.

SOLID SKILLS IN HAND-TO-HAND COMBAT CAN
BE AN AGENT'S GREATEST ASSET.

137
136
135
134
133
132
131
130
129
128
127
126
125
124
123
122
121
120
119

USE MOMENTUM TO BRING
DOWN YOUR OPPONENT.

150

149

148

147

146

145

144

143

142

141

140

139

138

137

136

135

134

133

132

131

130

129

128

127

126

125

124

123

122

USE MOMENTUM.

The physics of hand-to-hand combat plays a major role in the teachings of everything from tai chi to aikido. Harnessing momentum can give you extra power that can be redirected at your attacker, often with great success. Remember that momentum is not just generated from your own movement. The key to success is to harness your opponent's energy as well: Redirecting your opponent's lunges and take-downs, for example, can turn the tables effectively.

IDENTIFY, MOVE TOWARD, AND ATTACK YOUR OPPONENT'S WEAK SIDE.

One of the basic tenets of hand-to-hand combat is to identify and take advantage of your opponent's weak side. Watch the way your opponents move and which side they favor, then play to their weaknesses.

FOCUS ON EXISTING INJURIES.

It therefore follows from the prior strategy that any existing injuries your opponent has suffered should also be the focus of your attack. Your opponent's weak side may normally be on the right, but that all changes if your opponent has been injured on the left. Exploiting someone's injuries may feel strange or cruel to those of you who have fought almost exclusively in training scenarios. However, there is no such thing as a "fair fight" when you're fending off terrorist attacks. Just do what you need to do to get the job done.

KEEP YOUR INJURIES TO YOURSELF.

Everything you are planning to do to your opponent, your opponent is likely planning to do to you as well. It is of great advantage to train on both sides of your body, if possible, to make it more difficult for the hostile to identify your weak side—and you can be sure that your attacker will try to. If you happen to be injured in the course of combat, or if you are already dealing with an injury, do everything you can to keep it hidden—no matter how much more pain you have to endure.

AIM FOR PRESSURE POINTS.

The various types of hand-to-hand combat are, in essence, art forms that require years of dedication and a lifetime to master. Don't let your desire to show off your skills get in the way of immobilizing a hostile by whatever means possible. Act decisively and quickly, and remember to strike at pressure points. The knees, elbows, solar plexus, eyes, throat, kidneys, and, of course, genitals are all targets. Injuring any of these key areas can do enough damage and inflict enough pain to give you the upper hand, but will still enable you to bring a suspect in generally unharmed—or at least not in danger of imminent death. Remember, a living hostile may be a useful hostile. Bringing in a hostile in a condition that will allow further interrogation is often more valuable to the mission than killing the individual—and the injury can be manipulated to encourage the sharing of information.

151
150
149
148
147
146
145
144
143
142
141
140
139
138
137
136
135
134
133
132
131
130
129
128
127
126
125
124
123

24 | SURVIVING IN THE LINE OF GUNFIRE

As you know from your weapons training course, it is difficult to become profi-
cient in gun skills. Indeed, most people who have not had adequate training
would find it hard to pick up a firearm, properly squeeze the trigger, and hit their
intended target. For all CTU agents, this is good news, because it means that
it is typically easy to evade gunfire from untrained persons. Even with training,
it is difficult to hit a specific target or a specific person who is practicing solid
gunfire evasion techniques. You must treat all gunfire incidents as potentially
lethal since you will not know at the outset the gunmen's degree of training. The
important thing is to stay alive—either by evading the attack or taking the hostiles out and completing your mission. Here's what to do.

ASSUME THAT THE SOUND YOU HEAR IS GUNFIRE.

Unfortunately, most civilians shrug off the first signs of a shooting incident, assuming the sounds are
firecrackers. This assumption gets them into trouble because they continue about their business until
they blunder into a stray bullet or the actual shooter. At the first sound of "firecrackers," assume you
are dealing with gunfire.

GET DOWN—ALL THE WAY DOWN.

A hostile who is randomly spraying cover fire will be standing at his or her full height. You want to be
below the bullets' trajectory, so you must drop flat to the ground. Once there, you can better assess the
situation and determine your next step.

RUN TO ESCAPE.

Wait for silence. The hostile may be reloading, switching to a new weapon, moving to a new position,
or sighting new targets. The farther away from the weapon you are, the greater your chances of survival.
Even experienced snipers have trouble striking a moving target at a distance. So run, but not in a
straight line. A straight retreat makes it easier for a shooter to predict your next move. Make it harder
by running in a serpentine path.

IF YOU'RE UNDER FIRE, STAY CLOSE TO THE GROUND.

152
151
150
149
148
147
146
145
144
143
142
141
140
139
138
137
136
135
134
133
132
131
130
129
128
127
126
125
124

RUN AROUND A CORNER.

Bullets cannot turn corners. If bullets are flying, the quickest way to attain safety is to make a swift right or left turn around a building or large object. Unless you intend to return fire, it serves no purpose to look back around the corner to locate the shooter(s). Just keep moving or hide. On rooftops, a chimney or smokestack structure makes an adequate "corner." In the wild, a thick tree will serve the same purpose. Holes in the ground are another option, but remember that an unstopped bullet's ultimate destination is the ground.

Use solid objects to protect yourself. The heavier and more solid an object is, the better chance it has of stopping a bullet. Concrete and steel are excellent, but most other building materials, such as Sheetrock, interior doors, or thick panel glass, are not. If you take shelter near a car, hide behind the front of the car. Most parts of a car can be easily penetrated, but the engine block will stop a bullet cold. (Unfortunately, if the engine is running, it may ignite if struck.) SUVs and most civilian trucks may look solid, but they are just as vulnerable; they also offer less protection because they sit higher off the ground.

153
152
151
150
149
148
147
146
145
144
143
142
141
140
139
138
137
136
135
134
133
132
131
130
129
128
127
126
125

CLEAR THE AREA OF CIVILIANS AND UNTRAINED AGENTS.

Once you are safely hidden, you can better attend to the needs of innocent bystanders. Depending on the circumstances, you may have to do so solely by voice or hand signals. Make sure they heed your instructions to clear the area, stay down, take cover, and so forth. Attend to the wounded and dead after you have eliminated the threat.

DRAW OUT AND ELIMINATE THE HOSTILE.

If you are a field agent who must complete his or her mission, by all means commence fire as soon as you reach adequate cover. Use the techniques discussed above to move across the terrain to your destination. Whenever possible, try to draw your assailant out of cover. It helps to create a diversion, such as lobbing a grenade at a distant structure or attacker. Alternatively, you may be able to simulate the sound of gunfire by placing a few of your own rounds in a can, lighting it, and running away. The sounds will camouflage your true position, as your attacker will fire back directly at your diversion, leaving the path clear for you to move to a better position, draw closer to the hostile's position, or take higher ground.

OTHER TACTICS

Be aware that flashlights or other bright lights can blind or disorient attackers equipped with night-vision goggles. (The same applies to you if you're employing night vision equipment.)

Always clear weapons, clips, and ammo away from dead or surrendered hostiles and collect them for further use.

If you have a partner, work as a team. Your partner may have a point of view or perspective on the action that you lack. Let your partner spot the shooter, reveal the hostile's position, and then cover you as you go in for the kill.

An analyst on the floor at CTU can act as your partner as well, provided he or she can access satellite or thermal scans of the area.

Be aware that some weapons manufacturers and terrorist organizations are experimenting with detonating bullets. Even if you turn a corner, the bullet could explode just as it passes you and take you out. We have not seen use of this technology in the field, but it may soon become a reality.

154
153
152
151
150
149
148
147
146
145
144
143
142
141
140

BASIC SNIPER TRAINING WILL HELP
YOU UNDERSTAND THE WEAPON'S
STRENGTHS AND LIMITATIONS.

139
138
137
136
135
134
133
132
131
130
129
128
127
126

E5   SPOTTING AND ELIMINATING A SNIPER

In military parlance, a sniper is a highly trained professional marksman who is dispatched alone to perform a vital role in field reconnaissance and to take out important targets from a secure, hidden position. True field snipers use long-range weapons equipped with bolt-action and try to fire as few shots as possible to take out a target. It is extremely difficult to become a certified sniper—or even a short-range sharpshooter—in any of the world's military or paramilitary forces.

On occasion, CTU field and intelligence agents may draw fire from individuals in hidden locations. We hesitate to call these individuals snipers since the term suggests a level of skill that these hostiles may not possess. More often

155
154
153
152
151
150
149
148
147
146
145
144
143
142
141
140
139
138
137
136
135
134
133
132
131
130
129
128
127

we encounter individuals with a wide range of marksmanship skills (excellent to poor) using an assault rifle from a hidden location. This does not mean you should discount the very real danger of being fired upon by an unseen or invisible enemy. Urban combat is theoretically more dangerous than an attack in a natural setting. In the open field it is still possible to pick up visual and auditory clues that may reveal a hidden shooter's position. In the urban environment, this is more difficult because manmade structures consisting of glass, steel, concrete, and asphalt all reverberate and hamper detection. But you still may be able to use your excellent training and CTU resources to locate and take out the hostile based on the following tips.

IF YOU ARE ALONE AND UNDER FIRE

TAKE COVER AND ANALYZE. At the first sign of gunfire, take cover and quickly scan nearby rooftops or open windows. Try to determine the skill level of the shooter, based on behavior. True snipers are trained in precision fire and will be extremely selective about the number of rounds fired. If the shooter is wantonly spraying bullets, you are not under fire by a true sniper. Use this trigger-happy tendency against the hostile. If the shots are slow, methodical, and unpredictable, occurring several minutes apart, then you may be dealing with a well-camouflaged, highly trained opponent. In this case, restrain your movements or freeze altogether while planning your next move.

SEEK SATELLITE SURVEILLANCE. As soon as possible, contact a CTU intelligence agent and request satellite surveillance of the area. A thermal scan will pinpoint the precise location of the shooter, and you will be better able to return fire.

ANALYZE THE AZIMUTH. If satellite surveillance is unavailable, try to determine the azimuth, or the direction of the shots, by studying the angle or elevation as suggested by bullet holes in the area. The easiest way to do so is to insert a dowel, extendable-mirror handle, or other thin, straight stick into a hole and then note which way the stick points. Admittedly, this task is extremely difficult while under fire, but the shooter may have hit a structure, vehicle, or other stationary object near you that can be safely analyzed.

156
155
154
153
152
151
150
149
148
147
146
145
144
143
142
141
140

EXPLOIT VISUAL AND ACOUSTIC EVENTS. Scan the area for clues to your attacker's position. Muzzle flashes, the reflection of a rifle scope, and the sound of rifle fire may help pinpoint the hostile's location.

AN EFFECTIVE SNIPER CAN USE HIS WEAPON IN VIRTUALLY ANY SETTING.

THINK LIKE A SNIPER. If you have had sniper training, you will be able to put yourself in the mind of your opponent. Think: If I were setting up a shot in this environment, where would I situate my "hide"?

RECALL THE SHOOTER'S WEAKNESSES. True snipers have only two advantages: They're hidden, and they can use the element of surprise. If you can force them to move or fire more often, they will betray their position. (Untrained shooters will be easy to flush out on both these counts because they are more likely to panic, leave their position, and return fire while on the move.)

139
138
137
136
135
134
133
132
131
130
129
128

157
156
155
154
153
152
151
150
149
148
147
146
145
144
143
142
141
140
139
138
137
136
135
134
133
132
131
130
129

FIRE AND MOVE; FIRE AND LURE IN. Concentrate all your fire on the sniper's position, wait for him or her to return fire, and then—when you can safely manage it—change position. Seek to change your position so drastically that the hostile must move and rearrange the bipod to set up a new shot. The shooter is vulnerable when moving. Use this opportunity to eliminate the hostile.

BLIND THE ATTACKER. On Day 1, when Agent Bauer was being stalked in the woods by shooter Ira Gaines, he was able to successfully blind his attacker by angling a piece of metallic debris at him. This tactic worked in Bauer's case, but it could have easily revealed his position as well. You must act quickly when your attacker is momentarily blinded.

IF YOU ARE ACCOMPANIED BY A CTU TACTICAL TEAM WHILE UNDER FIRE

Follow the procedures outlined above. Be aware that CTU Tac is currently experimenting with a number of different countersniper technologies, with the cooperation of DARPA (Defense Advanced Research Projects Agency). At least fifteen different systems are currently in operation in the U.S. They work by using laser, sonar, or radar devices to track bullet trajectories. One such system, the wireless sensor network (WSN), works as follows:

- As the sniper's bullet is fired, a ballistic shockwave is produced as the supersonic bullet "cracks" the air.
- Wireless sonar devices attached to CTU vehicles, the helmets of Tac team members, and (in some Los Angeles neighborhoods) stationary cameras mounted on traffic poles capture the sound signature, break it down, and trace it back to its source, using complex algorithmic software.
- The sniper's location is pinpointed and sent to the PDAs of the three highest-ranking CTU officials on site.
- The technology employed changes semiannually, at the discretion of CTU's purchasing department and its liaison with the Department of Defense. Always familiarize yourself with the current system and know how it works. Remember that these devices are still in the experimental phase and are not foolproof.

158
157
156
155
154
153
152
151
150
149
148
147
146
145
144
143
142
141
140
139
138
137
136
135
134
133
132
131
130
129

E6 — TREATING KNIFE AND BULLET WOUNDS

Serious injury is a potential likelihood for any member of the CTU. An injury to yourself or others in the field must be addressed quickly and efficiently, with minimum risk to the mission. A CTU operative in the field rarely has the same options available to other law-enforcement agencies. Calling for an ambulance is often not the best course of action, as standard channels of emergency medical treatment may compromise the mission. In the fight to neutralize terrorist elements, urban and suburban areas are war zones, and field injuries must be treated the same way they would under combat conditions. Hostile targets rarely subside long enough to allow you to call 9-1-1.

The CTU provides mandatory training in the field treatment of injuries. All new agents are required to pass this course. Failure to do so will result in your being restricted to desk duty until the requirement has been met. If you are seeking a field agent appointment and find you cannot stomach the sight of torn flesh on your own body or that of a fellow agent, speak to your supervisor about permanent reassignment. A mission is as successful as its weakest operative. In the field, if you are unprepared, you are a liability.

The following serves as a refresher for the emergency treatment of knife and gunshot wounds *only*. For more information on severed limbs and field amputations, refer to section E7 of the handbook (page 135).

The three main objectives for treating all penetrative wounds are:

- Stopping the flow of blood

- Preventing shock

- Staving off infection

159
158
157
156
155
154
153
152
151
150
149
148
147
146
145
144
143
142
141
140
139
138
137
136
135
134
133
132
131

1. ASSESS THE SITUATION, THEN THE WOUND.

If you are under fire, only when the threat is eliminated can you best attend to your wound or anyone else's. Seek cover, if possible, and then inspect any injuries. Recall that on Day 1, former administrative director Richard Walsh attended to his own gunshot wound to the forearm as Agent Bauer returned fire. Only after they retreated into the temporary safety of a stairwell was Bauer able to bind his partner's wound with a necktie. If there are multiple casualties, follow triage procedure.

2. EXPOSE THE WOUND. STOP THE BLEEDING.

Remove any garments or protective gear to expose the wound so that the appropriate dressing can be applied. Apply direct pressure to the area and elevate, if the situation permits. Remove any gross debris, if loose. Do not remove any lodged foreign objects from the wound. It is often possible to stop mild to moderate bleeding through elevation, pressure, and a quick field dressing. Applying pressure to the body's pressure points—where a major artery feeding the site of injury is close to the surface of the skin and directly over a bone—can stem a good deal of bleeding. There are twenty-two such pressure points throughout the body, but three to remember are the brachial, femoral, and carotid arteries.

If bleeding cannot be controlled by pressure and you are on the move, a tourniquet should be applied to prevent loss of consciousness—or life—due to rapid blood loss. Though tourniquets are regarded as a last resort, in the field they can be a quick, acceptable way to stop heavy bleeding so that you can deal with other attackers and immediate physical threats. CTU field agents under fire often do not have the luxury of lying down and elevating a wound. Ties, belts, nylons/stockings, and shirtsleeves can all be used. Bear in mind, however, that tourniquets often do more damage to a limb than other pressure dressings. Do not, especially in the case of gunshot injuries, attempt to close the wound. Gunpowder and clothing that have been introduced into the body cavity by the shot will be more likely to fester and cause infection when closed. Tourniquets should not be removed once they are applied. Wait until a medical professional can attend to the injury.

I M P O R T A N T

Under no circumstances should a blood-soaked bandage be removed and replaced with a fresh one. Simply place the new bandage over the existing one and follow standard dressing procedures as demonstrated by your instructors at the CTU clinic.

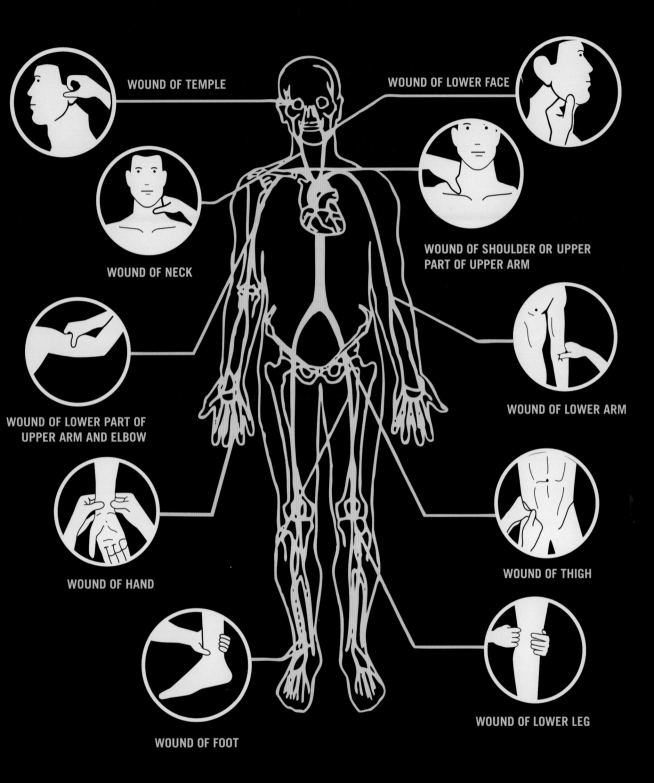

WOUND OF TEMPLE

WOUND OF LOWER FACE

WOUND OF NECK

WOUND OF SHOULDER OR UPPER PART OF UPPER ARM

WOUND OF LOWER PART OF UPPER ARM AND ELBOW

WOUND OF LOWER ARM

WOUND OF HAND

WOUND OF THIGH

WOUND OF FOOT

WOUND OF LOWER LEG

USE PRESSURE POINTS TO SLOW THE LOSS OF BLOOD.

161
160
159
158
157
156
155
154
153
152
151
150
149
148
147
146
145
144
143
142
141
140
139
138
137
136
135
134
133

IN EXTREME SITUATIONS, MANY VIC-TIMS OF SERIOUS INJURY WILL PROVE TO BE SURPRISINGLY RESILIENT.

3. DO NOT PUSH PROTRUDING ORGANS BACK INTO THE BODY CAVITY.

Doing so may result in more extensive injury to the organs, as bone fragments or foreign objects may further damage the tissue. Cover the area with a damp dressing. A dry dressing may in fact draw excessive blood or critical body fluids out of the damaged organ, increasing the likelihood of death.

162

161

160

159

158

157

156

155

154

153

152

151

150

149

148

147

146

145

144

143

142

141

140

139

138

137

136

135

134

4. AVOID SELF-MEDICATION.

The self-administration of painkillers or other pharmaceuticals beyond antiseptics and anal-gesics should be avoided during an active threat. They will affect your reaction time and pos-sibly impair your judgment.

5. REDUCE THE POTENTIAL FOR SHOCK.

Ensure the airway is open. If possible, lay the injured individual on his or her back and elevate the feet. Keep the individual warm and calm and discourage excessive movement.

6. CAUTERIZE WOUNDS WHEN APPROPRIATE.

Under some circumstances, the cauterization of a serious wound may help stop the bleeding and kill bacteria. On Day 3, after Agent Edmunds was shot in the hand by members of the Salazar organization, he seared his open wound with a hot poker, knowing that it would likely be hours before he would be able to receive medical attention.

A NOTE ON TREATING HOSTILES

First, disarm the suspect and stow his or her weapon. Then treat the suspect's wound as you would your own or a fellow agent's. If the suspect appears near death, glean any and all information before releas-ing the individual for medical treatment. For subjects who display a good chance of survival, bear in mind that this opportunity may allow you to build a trust that could pay off during a later interrogation. As much as you may find it distasteful to administer care to a hostile—especially one who has just tried to dispose of you—remember the big picture. A noncommittal "Hang in there" will suffice. State also that you have requested medical assistance.

I M P O R T A N T

We cannot stress enough that the severely injured need to be kept in a secure position and as free from movement as possible. That will accomplish two things: First, it reduces the likeli-hood of increased injury from excessive bleeding and the disruption of healing coagulation. Second—and perhaps more important—sudden movements may draw additional fire, which will serve only the needs of the hostile. Consider again Walsh's demise on Day 1. Against Bauer's instructions, Walsh passed an encoded key card to him, and his flailing arms made him an easy target.

143
142
141
140
139
138
137
136
135

It is not always in the best interest of the operation to stay at the scene with deceased team members. However, all deaths should be called into CTU immediately so that the bodies can be collected and the scene secured for further investigation.

WHENEVER POSSIBLE, STAY WITH THE INJURED UNTIL SUPPORT ARRIVES.

164

163

162

161

160

159

158

157

156

155

154

153

152

151

150

TREATING A SEVERED LIMB

As a federal agent, you are expected to weather a crisis without allowing it to derail a mission. When disaster strikes, we don't have the option to take time out from stopping terrorists in their tracks. Nothing must take priority over the mission, no matter how serious it seems. Dealing with injuries to your colleagues or yourself during combat must take place as swiftly as possible. However, there are few things that will unnerve even the most seasoned agents more than the sight of a severed limb.

Severed limbs can result from any number of situations, from car accidents to torture. The good news is that severed limbs can be reattached successfully. Early attention and treatment are crucial. Time is of the essence, of course, and a cool head can mean the difference between life and death.

The severing of a limb is usually accidental. In these cases, the severing will most likely not be neat, and it may also be incomplete. In a major accident, do your best to locate *all* severed body parts. No part is too small.

Under extenuating circumstances, it may become necessary to sever a limb on purpose—for example, if you attach a detonator containing a deadly biovirus to your wrist. The titanium dispersal unit that Agent Edmunds attached to his wrist on Day 3 contained the deadly Cordilla virus. Unfortunately, Edmunds felt his action was necessary to prevent the terrorist from escaping with the virus and causing an outbreak in Los Angeles. It may also be necessary to perform a self-amputation to escape from a life-threatening situation.

149

148

147

146

145

144

143

142

141

140

139

138

137

136

165
164
163
162
161
160
159
158
157
156
155
154
153
152
151
150
149
148
147
146
145
144
143
142
141
140
139
138
137

AFTER THE AMPUTATION

No matter how the limb has been severed, the treatment goals are similar to those for other wounds: control the bleeding, stave off infection, and prevent the onset of shock. First, make sure the subject is breathing and that CPR is not necessary, then address the wound.

STOP THE BLEEDING. If possible, elevate the affected area. Applying direct pressure is the preferred way to stop the bleeding, but if the bleeding is life threatening—which it may be if a major artery has been severed—a tourniquet should be administered to prevent death by loss of blood. (For more information about tourniquets, see E6, "Treating Knife and Bullet Wounds," page 129.) If a major artery has been severed, death can occur in as few as two to three minutes. Once a tourniquet is applied, do not remove it until medical help is available. With a complete amputation, there will often be little or no bleeding because the blood vessels constrict and pull back into the body. However, if a major artery is severed and immediate medical attention is not available, it may still be advisable to apply a tourniquet because, once the vessels have relaxed, bleeding will resume. For partial hand or foot amputation, bleeding may be stopped through elevation and the application of direct pressure.

ASSESS OTHER INJURIES. Although controlling the bleeding at the site of the amputation is the first priority, be sure not to overlook other significant wounds that may need immediate attention. Not all such injuries are as obvious as a severed limb, but that does not mean they are any less serious. So, once the bleeding has been controlled, be sure to carefully inspect the body.

PREVENT SHOCK. Keep the subject calm. This objective may be more challenging than in other injury situations, as the sight of a severed limb is extremely jarring. Speak calmly. Avoid any discussion of the reattachment of the limb. Place the subject on his or her back and raise the feet roughly twelve inches above the ground, unless other injuries make this inadvisable. Be sure you do not move a person suspected of suffering a back or neck injury, or if moving makes the subject uncomfortable or causes pain. As with all shock patients, cover the subject with a blanket or coat.

KEEP THE INJURY CLEAN. Gently wipe or rinse off any obvious debris. Remove any obvious debris from the wound. Use sterile dressings if available.

HANDLE THE SEVERED LIMB WITH CARE. The limb should be kept cool, but it should not be frozen or come into contact with ice, which can permanently damage the tissue. If

166
165
164
163
162
161
160
159
158
157
156
155
154
153
152
151
150
149
148
147
146
145
144
143
142
141
140
139
138

ON VERY RARE OCCASIONS, THE DELIBERATE AMPUTA-
TION OF A LIMB MAY BE YOUR BEST COURSE OF ACTION.

possible, cover it with a sterile, damp cloth; place it in an airtight bag; and submerge the bag in cold or iced water. Do *not* submerge the limb directly in water. If you lack access to ice or cold water or a bag, do your best to place a clean, damp cloth around the limb and keep it away from heat sources. With proper cooling, a limb may be viable up to eighteen hours. Without proper cooling, that time shrinks to four to six hours.

SPLINT PARTIAL AMPUTATIONS. If the amputation is partial, splint the limb. Do your best to stop the bleeding by applying direct pressure, but be particularly careful not to cut off the bleeding to the rest of the limb. If you do, you will negate any possibility of success-ful reattachment. As always, if bleeding is life-threatening, do what is necessary to stop it.

167
166
165
164
163
162
161
160
159
158
157
156
155
154
153
152
151
150
149
148
147
146
145
144
143
142
141
140
139

E8   SURVIVING IN AN EXPLOSION

Explosions can be some of the most damaging and destructive weapons in the terrorist arsenal. They can destroy lives, information, and evidence. Bombing is, statistically, the most frequently used tactic in terrorist attacks. Even when an explosive device is spotted ahead of time, there may not always be enough time to call in the bomb squad to defuse or dismantle the explosive device. (For more information on disposing of a live bomb, see section G3, page 182.) Explosions may result from a variety of causes: planted plastic explosives, grenades, car bombs, or suicide bombers. If you are trapped in a confined space with a powerful bomb, there is obviously no guarantee—and little chance—that you can completely avoid serious harm or death. Depending on the situation and the available time, there are several steps you can take to minimize your injuries and possibly save your life.

IF DETONATION IS IMMINENT

If a grenade has been thrown or a suicide bomber is about to detonate his or her package, drop to the ground and protect your head and vital organs. (See "Protect Yourself," page 141.)

IF THERE IS TIME BEFORE DETONATION

If a bomb has been planted and wired to explode within a specific time frame, take advantage of every available moment.

DISTANCE YOURSELF FROM THE BOMB. If you know where the bomb is, put as much distance as you can between you and the impending explosion. If you know how much time is left before detonation, run as far and as fast as possible and do your best to reach cover before the explosion. If you are in a large, open space and cannot secure adequate cover before the blast, protect yourself as described below.

168
167
166
165
164
163
162
161
160
159
158
157
156
155
154
153
152
151
150
149
148

MAXIMIZE THE DISTANCE BETWEEN
YOURSELF AND THE EXPLOSION.

PLACE OBSTACLES BETWEEN YOU AND THE EXPLOSIVE DEVICE. If the bomb is in an adjoining room, close and blockade the door with large objects, such as file cabinets, tables, or chairs. Be aware, of course, that anything you place in the path of the blast can become a dangerous projectile. A door may be blown off its hinges, for example, and come hurtling your way.

TAKE COVER. Get under or behind any available object—a table or door—or move around a corner from the explosion. If there is nothing sturdy to hide behind or under, place a blanket or coat over your head to protect your eyes from flying debris.

147
146
145
144
143
142
141
140

169
168
167
166

162

160
159
158
157
156
155
154
153
152
151
150
149
148
147
146
145
144
143
142
141

USE ANY NATURAL OR MAN-MADE
OBJECT TO SHIELD YOURSELF
FROM THE BLAST.

PROTECT YOURSELF. Whether or not you are able to take cover, do your best to protect your head and vital organs. If you are in the open and within close proximity to the explosion, drop to the ground and position yourself so that your head is away from the origin of the blast. Lie flat on your stomach, with your elbows held tight at your sides, to protect your organs. Cover your ears and head with your hands.

170

169

168

167

166

165

164

163

162

161

160

159

158

157

156

155

154

153

152

151

150

149

148

147

146

145

144

143

142

SPECIAL CIRCUMSTANCES

If a hostile is holding a grenade or other bomb in a crowded public area, it may be possible to take the hostile down, falling on the hostile and the grenade and using the hostile to shield you and any innocent bystanders from the blast. The explosion may send you flying, but the hostile and the ground should sustain most of the damage.

Use the terrorist's weapon against the perpetrator. On Day 5, hostages were taken at the Ontario Airport by terrorists clothed in vests wired with explosives. Agents Bauer and O'Brian realized that one of the detonators on the vests was wireless and likely controlled by the lead terrorist. Bauer's cell phone was then successfully reconfigured to the detonator's frequency, and Bauer was able to explode the vest—and the hostile wearing it—from behind closed doors. This outcome confused and disoriented the hostiles, striking terror and fear into the terrorists themselves.

Shield your eyes and ears. Damage to hearing can be serious and permanent, and debris in your eyes can blind you. Case in point: On Day 5, Agent Bauer found himself in close proximity to a bomb that was about to detonate, and he was forced to use a variety of these techniques to survive. Bauer was trying to take down former CTU director and Omicron executive Christopher Henderson, who was involved in a conspiracy with President Charles Logan to provide Sentox nerve gas to terrorist groups. Henderson locked Bauer in a bunker with a bomb set to detonate in mere moments. With no escape route or windows, Bauer quickly barricaded the bomb location and loosened a tile from the floor. He managed to crawl under the floor and seek cover there until the blast had passed. His quick thinking paid off, and he sustained minimal injuries.

F | INTERROGATION

INFORMATION IS OUR MOST VALUABLE CURRENCY AT CTU: GETTING IT, VETTING IT, AND ACTING ON IT JUDICIOUSLY ARE THREE TASKS THAT FORM THE BASIS OF ALL OUR MOST IMPORTANT OPERATIONS. NO TWO INTERROGATIONS WILL BE ALIKE, BECAUSE NO TWO SUBJECTS ARE THE SAME. INTERROGATION IS A BATTLE OF WILLS, BUT ONE THAT MUST REMAIN FREE OF OVERBLOWN EGOS. EXPERIENCE IS THE ONLY TEACHER HERE, BUT THE STUDENT MUST BE WILLING TO LEARN—EVEN FROM KNOWN TERRORISTS. SEVERAL TECHNIQUES CAN HELP KEEP YOU ON THE RIGHT TRACK AND BETTER ENABLE YOU TO ACQUIRE—OR PROTECT—THE INFORMATION THAT SAFEGUARDS THE LIVES OF THE AMERICAN PEOPLE.

173
172
171
170
169
168
167
166
165
164
163
162
161
160
159
158
157
156
155

INTERROGATING SUSPECTS

Information is everything—especially when you're scrambling to save millions of lives from well-funded, highly motivated, nonlinear enemies. CTU rarely has the luxury of lengthy investigations, wiretaps, or stakeouts. As former SAC George Mason once told a Congressional Oversight Committee, "You call the FBI if someone's building a bomb. You call us if they've already lit the fuse."

A few minutes of grilling a suspect can yield as much intelligence as weeks—even months—of fieldwork, if you know what you're doing. But the same charter that gives us the responsibility to protect America from terrorists also limits the methods we can use to interrogate them. In light of recent allegations by the media of "torture," as well as several high-profile civil suits brought against CTU by former detainees, the agency is constantly revising our guidelines and acceptable tactics.

The following are general interrogation guidelines. For additional tips on handling high-profile subjects and seasoned terrorists, see section F3.

154
153
152
151
150
149
148
147
146
145

PREPARE THE HOLDING ROOM.

It is preferable to conduct interrogations on CTU property, but that is not always feasible. At CTU, we have the ability to monitor breathing and blood pressure, conduct iris scans, refer to a lie detector, and record an audio-visual account of the event for later scrutiny. Stow your weapons before entering the room. Also, be sure that your suspect has a chair—he or she should remain seated during the interrogation (and, if necessary, be forcibly restrained). Finally, check to make sure that any technology and monitoring devices you will be using are performing properly. Review all relevant intelligence.

DEMAND THE NECESSARY INFORMATION.

Tell your suspect that he or she has one—and only one—opportunity to provide the information you need. Maintain eye contact and do not smile. It may help to suggest that you already have the information and that you are simply giving the suspect a chance to tell his or her side of the story. Add a bit of

174
173
172
171
170
169
168
167
166
165
164
163
162
161
160
159
158
157
156
155
154
153

MAINTAIN EYE CONTACT AND INVADE A SUBJECT'S PER-
SONAL SPACE TO ACCELERATE THE INTERROGATION.

drama: Announce that the monitoring devices are recording and that the torture specialist is on standby. You can effectively create an air of suspense before even asking the first question.

MAINTAIN YOUR STATE.

Stay in a cognitive rather than emotional state of mind. That is the best way to retain control of an interrogation. If you are going to use an emotion, such as anger, to coerce a subject, use it wisely. Always monitor who is in control. There are times when it is advantageous to let your subjects think they have bested you. It can help them to relax, become sloppy, and inadvertently give up information. At other times, interrogation subjects may be rather pleased that they have information that you need. They will feel as though they are trifling with you. It is up to you to let them know that they are not.

152
151
150
149
148
147
146

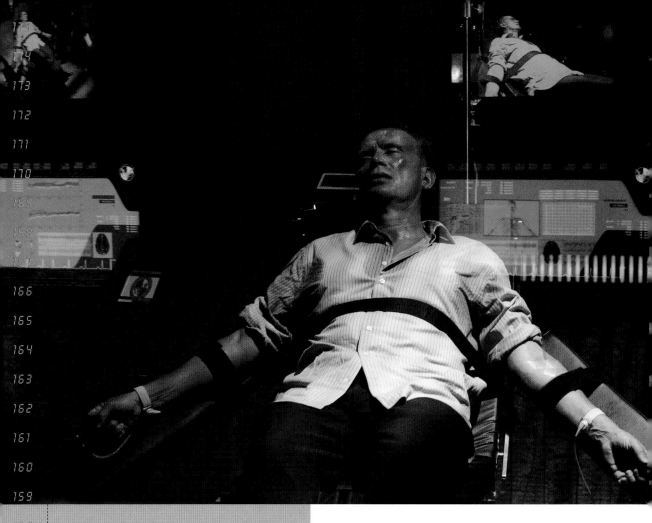

173

172

171

170

169

168

167

166

165

164

163

162

161

160

159

155

154

153

152

151

150

149

148

147

146

IN SPECIAL CIRCUMSTANCES, CTU CAN OFFER
NONLETHAL CHEMICAL ASSISTANCE TO EXPEDITE
AN INTERROGATION.

OFFER HYPOTHETICAL EMPATHY.

Tell the suspect that you're sorry it had to happen like this, but you have no choice. You're sure he's a reasonable individual. Ease him into feeling comfortable by identifying with his motives and finding common ground. You might try reasoning with the subject: "I can see you care about your son. Let us help you help keep him safe. Cooperate." Of course, this tactic may not work on more experienced subjects. Take former CTU director Christopher Henderson, for example. On Day 5, Henderson openly mocked Agent Bauer's attempts at empathy: "That's right, Jack. Disarm your subject's resolve by showing empathy and respect for his agenda."

INVADE PERSONAL SPACE.

Minimize the physical distance between you and the suspect. Americans are accustomed to 18–48 inches of "personal space" in conversations, and reducing this space will disorient the suspect. (Note that these measurements vary by culture: Many Russians, for example, are comfortable speaking across a distance of a mere 6–12 inches.)

176
175
174
173
172
171
170
169
168
167
166
165
164
163
162
161
160
159
158
157
156
155
154
153
152
151
150
149
148

TURN UP THE HEAT IN THE ROOM.

Physical discomfort adds to stress levels, and you can allude to the individual's profuse sweating as proof of his or her guilt or that he or she is holding out.

WATCH FOR VISUAL "TELLS."

Is the suspect exhibiting nonverbal signs of nervousness or deception? These include constantly shifting position, slouching, avoiding eye contact, crossing arms or legs, and swallowing or licking the lips. These signals help you determine if a suspect is telling the truth.

KNOW YOUR SUBJECT AND REALIZE THAT HE OR SHE MAY KNOW YOU.

"I know what you're thinking, Jack. The Bosnian secret police worked on me for two years and couldn't break me. Do you really think you'll be able to do it in less than an hour?" Bioterrorist and former MI6 agent Stephen Saunders spoke these words to Agent Bauer on Day 3. Saunders raised a good point, and it is one that you may need to ask yourself in the course of interrogation, especially under time constraints. You must be realistic about who you are interrogating and if the interrogation is the best use of your time.

ASK UNRELATED QUESTIONS; GET PERSONAL.

Personal information can be used to throw your subject off guard—use it. Also, random personal questions can cause your subject to let down his or her guard. Mix questions that are relevant to the case with those that are completely unrelated. If you're lucky, this non-sequitur approach will lead the suspect to slip up.

BE AWARE THAT THE SUBJECT MAY NOT REALIZE HE OR SHE HAS INFORMATION YOU WANT.

If so, it will take you even longer to get it. Richard, Secretary of Defense James Heller's son, had information vital to the apprehension of Habib Marwan on Day 4, but he simply didn't realize its significance. "I am not going to tell these people things about my private life that they don't need to know," he told his father. To which Secretary Heller responded, "That you don't *think* they need to know." Unfortunately, the younger Heller's actions cost CTU time, jeopardized his nation, and subjected him to passive torture techniques.

NEVER OFFER TO CUT A DEAL.

Neither you nor your SAC has the authority to offer a written presidential pardon (for more information on this point, see section F5, page 161). Do not offer money, political asylum, new identities, or other forms of protection. These offers will be perceived only as signs of weakness.

177
176
175
174
173
172
171

KNOW WHEN TO REQUEST A TORTURE SPECIALIST.

It is common for interrogations to last twelve to eighteen hours or more. At CTU, you may often find your-self in a situation where time is of the essence. In these cases, consider requesting a torture specialist. This person is trained in medicine and will use calibrated doses of pain to extract the necessary informa-tion. For more information about acceptable uses of excessive force, see section F4 (page 157).

170
169
168
167
166
165
164
163
162
161
160
159
158
157
156
155
154

F2   *WITHSTANDING INTERROGATION*

There is a very real possibility that, during your time as a part of the CTU team, you will be subjected to interrogation. As a CTU agent, you are well aware that your ability to maintain composure and protect information vital to the safety and security of the United States of America is paramount to our success. However, if you have never been subjected to extensive interrogation or extreme measures of coercion, you may not realize how tempted you will be to give up that information. We have a saying here at CTU: "Everyone breaks." The question you must therefore ask yourself is: "What is my break-ing point?"

This section is, in many ways, the reverse of the preceding section. Everything you have been trained to do as an interrogator is likely to be used against you. The good news is that, as an astute interrogator, you will be well versed in the likely techniques. The bad news is that you will be on the receiv-ing end of these unpleasant methods.

CONTROL YOUR EMOTIONS.

Just as agents seek to maintain an even keel while interrogating hostiles, so must they seek to remain in a cognitive, rather than an emotional, state when under interrogation. Keep in mind what you would do were the roles reversed, and then use that knowledge to beat your captor at his or her own game. If you find yourself becoming emotionally unhinged, do your best to channel your feelings into anger.

178
177
176
175
174
173
172
171
170
169
168
167
166
165
164
163
162
161
160
159
158
157
156
155
154
153
152
151
150

EVEN THE BEST FIELD AGENTS—LIKE THE LATE CURTIS MANNING—HAVE BEEN CAPTURED AND INTERRO-
GATED BY TERRORISTS. WITH PROPER TRAINING, YOU'LL BE PREPARED.

179
178
177
176
175
174
173
172
171
170
169
168
167
166
165
164
163
162
161
160
159
158
157
156
155
154
153
152
151

Nothing will encourage your captors more than fear—they can smell it. If remaining detached is out of the question, anger is the next best choice.

CHANGE THE GAME.

Do your best to disarm your interrogator. Remaining silent, stoic, and unmoved can be your best defense; however, throwing your interrogators off the trail may be an option if you have, for example, personal information about them and insight into their agenda. This technique is difficult but valuable. A good example of this tactic is taken from Day 3, when former CTU agent and traitor Nina Myers was interrogated by Agent Almeida regarding the whereabouts of bioterrorist Marcus Alvers. Myers immediately sought to unnerve Agent Almeida by asking about his wife and referring to her past personal relationships with both him and Agent Bauer. Though Almeida ultimately obtained his information, Myers's steely technique temporarily stalled the proceedings.

SEND THE WRONG SIGNALS.

Just as you would read the visual "tells" of a subject you are interrogating, you can use your own body language as a means to throw off your captors and send conflicting signals. Practice controlling your heart rate and breathing and be aware of your eye contact. Your ability to mask the body's natural responses can give you an edge. You can also use visual tells to offer invalid information and let the interrogators think they are extracting valuable information from you.

For example, should you decide to feign "giving in" and provide false information to your captors, be sure to appear relaxed and maintain eye contact. If necessary, look up to your right while speaking, which indicates an attempt to remember facts. Avoid looking up to your left, which indicates an attempt to fabricate information.

GIVE INCOMPLETE, INCORRECT, OR OUTDATED INFORMATION.

As an interrogation proceeds, if threats are made and force is used, you will undoubtedly be tempted to give up the information requested to halt the proceedings. If you find your resistance is wearing thin and you feel the need to speak, make an effort to offer information that is as useless to your captors as possible. Under these circumstances the most important thing is to "sell it": Make it seem as though you do not want to give up this information, but you can't hold out any longer. Trained interrogators will be able to easily spot someone who is trying to supply false facts. A good technique is to offer outdated details, information that was once "true." Speaking a form of "truth" can sometimes cause your body to behave as though you are telling the truth and, possibly, trick your captors as well.

REMEMBER THAT NO PIECE OF INFORMATION IS TOO SMALL.

Although you may think you know what information your captors are after, you must remember that your

180
179
178
177
176
175
174
173
172
171
170
169
168
167
166
165

assumptions could be completely wrong. You must vigilantly guard any and all information, no matter how insignificant you believe it to be. It just may be the piece of information the hostiles seek.

ALL CTU INTERROGATIONS ARE RECORDED AND ARCHIVED FOR FURTHER REVIEW.

STAY FOCUSED ON THE ENDGAME.

While undergoing interrogation, your mind can be your worst enemy. That is why you must bravely guard the gates of your own psyche. You may feel as though you have failed, simply by virtue of having been captured. You may feel that you are not strong enough, that you are succumbing to the pressure and therefore doing disservice to your colleagues and the citizens of the United States. You must not allow such thoughts to enter your mind and weaken your resolve. At CTU we take risks, and those risks include the possibility of being captured. If you do your best, capture does not reflect poorly on you. Remember that each moment you are able to hold out during an interrogation buys your colleagues valuable time. Your capture may be paramount to the overall success of the mission. There is no one person responsible. If we succeed, we succeed together. If we fail, we fail together. There's no room for self-deprecation and finger pointing: It's all about the team.

164
163
162
161
160
159
158
157
156
155
154
153
152
151

181
180
179
178
177
176
175
174
173
172
171
170
169
168
167
166
165
164
163
162
161
160
159
158
157
156
155
154
153
152

F3   HOW TO "TURN" A TERRORIST

During your tenure at CTU, you will encounter countless individuals who have devoted their lives to terrorizing innocent people as a means of promoting their own personal and political platforms. Although these individuals, these "terrorists," are the enemy, and you may despise everything they stand for and everything they do, you must ensure that your feelings do not interfere with your ability to perform your job. Extracting information from highly trained terrorists is one of the most important and most difficult tasks we undertake at CTU. The terrorists with whom we deal on a daily basis know exactly what's at stake; they are very capable of derailing even the most diligent and sophisticated attempts to extract information. Do not believe, no matter how experienced you are, that turning a terrorist will be easy.

As distasteful and incomprehensible as the terrorists' actions may seem, your ability to understand their mind-set is the key to a successful interrogation. It is particularly difficult to deal with those whose ideology differs completely from your own. It is even more difficult to deal with individuals who have no ideology whatsoever—trained assassins with no allegiance, for example. If you do not know what such people value or what matters to them, it is virtually impossible to coerce them into giving you information.

Throughout interrogation procedures, keep the following two approaches in mind. At first, these may appear contradictory.

1. Remain detached.

2. Tune in to the feelings and priorities of the hostile.

TERRORIST DINA ARAZ AGREED TO
ASSIST CTU IN EXCHANGE FOR
PROTECTION OF HER SON BEHROOZ

182
181
180
179
178
177
176
175
174
173
172
171
170
169
168
167
166
165
164
163
162
161
160
159
158
157
156
155
154
153

RICK ALLEN ASSISTED IN THE KIDNAPPING OF KIM BAUER — THEN LATER HELPED HER ESCAPE.

184

183

182

181

180

179

178

177

176

175

174

173

172

171

170

169

168

167

166

165

164

163

162

161

160

159

158

157

156

RESPECT YOUR SUBJECT'S ABILITIES.

You may despise everything they stand for, but the individuals you will interrogate must not be under-estimated. The minute you assume that you know more than your subject, that you are intellectually superior, or that you will have an easy time "tricking" the subject into giving you what you want, you lose the battle and compromise the larger objective.

KNOW WHO YOU'RE DEALING WITH.

Experience will help you improve your skills as an interrogator. You will be able to better determine who can be broken and who has a resolve that will be difficult to crack. If time permits, learn everything you can about your subject. Research their backgrounds, their associates, their weaknesses. Processing this information will help you determine what your subject is, and is not, willing to do for his or her cause. Knowing what he or she is willing to do will help you refine your interrogation strategy.

Your ability to read subjects will improve with experience. On Day 2, for example, during the interrogation of Marie Warner, Agent Bauer's vast experience told him that Warner was not prepared to do absolutely anything for her cause. When Bauer confronted Warner with his assessment of her commitment and will, her confidence faltered and she inadvertently revealed that the nuclear bomb CTU was tracking was still located at the airfield.

Keep in mind that no matter how much you learn, and how you improve your skills, you should never allow your abilities to make you too comfortable. Self-assurance is important. Overconfidence is a liability.

IDENTIFY THE TERRORIST'S NEEDS AND PRIORITIES.

Every terrorist wants something. Every terrorist needs something. Identifying what those needs and wants are can help you get information. Although you may know the terrorist organization's stated platform and objectives, you may not know what the individual in front of you seeks. You may also not have time to find out. As Agent Bauer said to Habib Marwan on Day 4, in an effort to get him to cooperate and stop the detonation of the nuclear warhead: "The death and destruction of innocent life is a means to an end. Why don't we just skip to the end?" If you are running out of time—as is often the case at CTU—find out what they want and then determine if giving it to them is a worthwhile option.

FIND COMMON GROUND.

You may think you have nothing in common with the terrorist across the table from you, but you are almost certainly wrong. Put your emotions aside and use any and all available information to connect to your subject. You may have shared experiences: an abusive childhood, a betrayal by colleagues, the loss of a loved one to war. Identifying these commonalities may provide the leverage you require.

USE THEIR FEARS AND EMOTIONAL ATTACHMENTS AS LEVERAGE.

Everyone has a weakness, and those weaknesses are usually grounded in emotional attachment. You are working to find cracks in terrorists' ideological armor; present situations that prompt them to question, even momentarily, what they are doing and why. That is not easy. However, as with any other interrogation, family ties often serve a vital purpose. Terrorists are often more than willing to die for their cause—and may even welcome the opportunity—but many are reluctant to make choices that will cause pain and suffering to their family. Threatening family members is not CTU's preferred method of operating. However when seeking to coerce a terrorist's cooperation, it has been used—without a go-ahead from district—and achieved the desired results.

On Day 2, Agent Bauer successfully staged the killing of terrorist Syed Ali's children via streaming video, which finally forced the hardened terrorist to cooperate. On Day 3, when Agent Bauer threatened to expose Stephen Saunders's daughter to the deadly Cordilla virus, Saunders gave in and cooperated with CTU to stop other planned biological attacks. And, of course, on Day 4, terrorist Dina Araz chose to cooperate with CTU in exchange for immunity for her son Behrooz. Araz offered even more information and agreed to participate in an undercover sting operation alongside Agent Bauer when she was promised the opportunity to enter the witness protection program with her son.

I M P O R T A N T

CTU does not normally condone threatening the lives of innocent people to extract information. However, under extenuating circumstances, this tactic is effective, though it is imperative no one is harmed. Nevertheless, keep in mind that none of these techniques are to be employed without consent from the SAC. Any agent who attempts to put these methods into action without prior approval will be subject to severe disciplinary actions, possible dismissal, and potential legal action.

KNOW WHEN TO USE FORCE.

Many of the individuals you will encounter are no strangers to violence and have very possibly been subjected to torture. Many will have unusually high tolerance for pain. Research has shown that using force guarantees neither success nor accurate information. Excessive force should always be a last resort and should *never* be used without prior consent from your SAC. For more information on acceptable measures of excessive force, see section F4.

186
185
184
183
182
181
180
179
178
177
176
175
174
173
172
171
170
169
168
167
166
165
164
163
162
161
160
159
158

KNOW WHEN TO GIVE UP.

Don't let your ego prevent you from identifying an individual who will be virtually impossible to break in a reasonable period. Time is usually a precious commodity.

F4

EXCESSIVE FORCE: WHEN THE END JUSTIFIES THE MEANS

Each day, terrorists plot to wreak wanton violence upon the citizens of this nation. At times, it may be necessary for CTU agents to use excessive force—i.e., torture—to ensure the rapid conclusion of a mission. New agents sometimes find it difficult to comprehend or condone some of the methods the agency uses to carry out its interrogations. Torture is distasteful and rightfully deplored by all good citizens of the world. But the judicious use, or the threat, of torture can be an effective tool to extract information. What follows is CTU policy, with a number of caveats for new agents.

CTU accepts that, under certain unusual circumstances, excessive force during interrogations may be necessary to bring about the peaceful resolution of a crisis and ensure a low civilian casualty rate. You may disagree with this policy on a personal level, but you are expected to comply with it if you are leading interrogations. If you cannot comply, you will be dismissed not only from the interrogation but from the mission as well.

As discussed in section F1, any physical coercion on CTU premises will always be medically controlled, monitored by audio-visual means and by CTU personnel, and not permanently damaging.

CTU considers torture to be justified if (a) the information cannot be extracted any other way, and (b) time is limited. Situations meeting both criteria are extremely rare. The most frequent uses of torture have occurred in only six days in agency history; even on those occasions, serious mistakes were made, and disciplinary action was issued.

The agency distinguishes between two forms of excessive force:

- **Active/Invasive:** in which the subject's skin or body is struck, shocked, stimulated, or physically penetrated with injectibles or by weapons that inflict pain without breaking the skin, such as stun guns, defibrillators, and so on.

- **Passive/Noninvasive:** in which the subject is made to endure a mentally debilitating experience. This approach is best epitomized by sensory-disorientation technique (SDT).

Research has shown that torture has only limited effectiveness. Information gleaned in this manner is always suspect. People will say anything to avoid being hurt, regardless of the type or extent of the pain. Your job is to know your subject's limits and respect them. You will quickly learn that the threat of force is often more powerful than its use. Use as little force as possible to extract the information you need.

Be open to the possibility that you may be torturing an innocent person. Twice in recent agency history, CTU has wrongfully tortured its own employees and paid the price politically as well as ethically.

176

175

174

173

172

171

170

169

168

167

166

165

164

163

162

161

160

159

158

THE THREAT OF FORCE IS OFTEN
MORE POWERFUL THAN ITS USE.

THE EXCESSIVE TACTICS OF AGENT CURTIS MAN-
NING LED TO HIS UNFORTUNATE DEMISE ON DAY 6.

188
187
186
185
184
183
182
181
180
179
178
177
176
175
174
173
172
171
170
169
168
167
166
165
164
163
162
161
160

Consider the regrettable moment in Day 5 when Homeland Security chief Karen Hayes became convinced that Audrey Raines, the daughter of the Secretary of Defense, was leaking confidential information to terrorists. Hayes gave the order for Ms. Raines to be tortured, but CTU sources later confirmed
that Ms. Raines was innocent of all charges. This kind of mistake can irrevocably damage a suspect as
well as your career.

    If at any time you suspect the interrogation has gone too far, or information has arisen that appears
to exonerate the subject, cease all efforts immediately. Bring the matter to the attention of your SAC or
supervisor. In this respect, natural abhorrence to torture is your greatest ally.

189
188
187
186
185
184
183
182
181
180
179

I M P O R T A N T

It is understood by District that excessive-force interrogations are routinely used in the field and may go well beyond the scope of those conducted on CTU premises. Shocking subjects with a frayed lamp cord or shooting a subject in the kneecap may seem necessary while operating in the field and against the clock, when the lives of millions are at stake. However, such activities are unacceptable. It is agency policy to review reports of abuse on a case-by-case basis, with some understanding of the pressures of the field agent's job. Let experience and good judgment be your guides. You may believe the end justifies the means, but those means may still result in your suspension from duty.

METHODS OF EXCESSIVE FORCE

ACTIVE METHODS

INJECTIONS: CTU torture specialists use a quick-acting, quick-dissipating nerve agent that stimulates all nerve endings, creating a burning sensation. The chemical itself is on loan to the agency and is constantly being modified by researchers working under DARPA grants. At this time the name and chemical composition of the current drug variant has not been released to prevent our enemies from training their operatives to withstand its effects. The drug causes instant pain, then stops, leaving the subject unharmed after a short time. The only way to induce greater pain is to administer a larger dose or more frequent doses. In most cases, there is no trace of the chemical in the subject's body after two hours and no mark indicates invasion except a small puncture at the injection site. In the past, we have also used hyocine-pentothal as a "truth" serum, but it is not foolproof, as was demonstrated on Day 5, in the unfortunate case of former agent Christopher Henderson. Henderson was subjected to large doses of this drug and still managed not only to conceal information while under its effects, but to attack and kill Agent Almeida. Its use is currently on hold, pending further analysis of its properties.

STUN GUNS: Local law enforcement agencies nationwide use these so-called nonlethal weapons to administer a controlled electric shock to the bodies of attackers. Stunners can administer as much as 800,000 volts, causing the subject to lose balance and become disoriented as his or her muscles contract violently. Lactic acid builds up as blood sugar is depleted, and the subject's muscles exhaust themselves from overwork. The use of these weapons is considered controversial because they have been implicated in some deaths.

178
177
176
175
174
173
172
171
170
169
168
167
166
165
164
163
162
161

190
189
188
187
186
185
184
183
182
181
180
179
178
177
176
175
174
173
172
171
170
169
168
167
166
165
164
163
162

METHOD

RIENTATION TECHNIQUE (SDT): A subject who is blindfolded and exposed to cacophonous
nutes or hours will gradually lose all sense of time and become severely confused. If the
ghtweight and a strobe light is used, nausea can be induced. To end the agony, the sub-
y share any information he or she may have. This method works because sound and light
ainfully exhausting if they are ceaseless and unpredictable. CTU audio experts have in
several different soundtracks, particularly from the 1970s, that will drive even the most
to distraction. This technique is the perfect choice for interrogating high-profile or polit-
e persons. It was used on Day 4 to interrogate Richard Heller, who was implicated in the
his father, Secretary of Defense James Heller.

PARDONS: WHEN TO INVOLVE THE PRESIDENT

From time to time, a CTU field or intelligence agent may need to arrange for

a presidential pardon for a person or persons under interrogation. In such

instances, you will be expected to follow proper CTU protocol. You must under-

stand how this process works because, since the advent of overt terrorism in

the U.S., our agency—in concert with the White House and the Department

of Justice—has been rewriting the laws governing pardons and immunity.

The terms are often used interchangeably, but they are not the same.

Both transactional and use immunity may be offered by a prosecutor.

Transactional immunity protects a person from being prosecuted for a partic-

ular offense or group of offenses. It is usually offered to a minor figure to gain

his or her cooperation to ensnare a larger figure. (Example: a minor organ-

ized-crime figure turns state's witness to convict a more powerful crime

boss.) Use immunity prevents a prosecutor from using a person's prior testi-

mony against that same person in court.

FORMER CTU DIRECTOR CHRISTOPHER HENDER-
SON IS JUST ONE OF THE MANY CRIMINALS WHO
INSISTED ON A PRESIDENTIAL PARDON BEFORE
COOPERATING WITH OUR AGENTS.

192
191
190
189
188
187
186
185
184
183
182
181
180
179
178
177
176
175
174
173
172
171
170
169
168
167
166
165
164

By law, only the president of the United States can grant a pardon that forgives a convicted or yet-to-be prosecuted person of a federal crime and exempts that individual from further legal penalties. The president can also commute (shorten) a convicted person's sentence. The president is granted this privilege under the United States Constitution, Article II, Section 2, which reads: "The President . . . shall have power to grant reprieves and pardons for offenses against the United States, except in cases of impeachment."

The typical pardon-application process is lengthy and can take years or decades. A convicted person's attorney applies to the Office of the Pardon Attorney (OPA), which makes recommendations to the White House. The FBI confirms the accuracy of the felon's dossier. The president then chooses the candidates and grants pardons around Christmastime or close to the chief executive's last day in office. Contrary to public opinion, most pardoned persons are guilty and have been convicted of minor offenses, such as burglary, auto theft, stolen goods trafficking, and the like. All pardons granted under this system are made public and subject to scrutiny by the media and legal scholars for years. At any given time, the OPA's office has a backlog of more than 3,000 pardon applications.

The above information pertains to the "public" pardon process. In recent years, CTU and other agencies involved in national security have developed a "covert" system for fast-tracking pardons and commutations directly from the White House. These are granted to facilitate ongoing investigations; that is, when there is simply no other way to acquire the information needed to stop a security threat. In our experience, the more professional, intelligent, and experienced the criminal, the more likely he or she will ask for a full presidential pardon in exchange for critical information. If granted, this agreement will remain covert—it will never be made public—to protect the president and the White House from appearing to have capitulated to terrorist demands. Remember, it is U.S.—and CTU—policy *not* to negotiate with terrorists.

CTU protocols require that all covert arrangements proceed according to the steps below.

1. DISSUADE PRISONERS FROM REQUESTING A PARDON.

Our mission is to imprison these criminals, not to absolve them and allow them to go free. For this reason, deflect all initial requests with standard interrogation platitudes, such as, "A pardon is really not in your best interest—trust me. Your best bet is to cooperate with us right now . . ." "If you cooperate with us, we'll put in a good word with the prosecutor . . ." "A pardon is simply not applicable in your case." At all costs, avoid being the first to mention the words president, pardon, immunity—the person in custody must be the one to raise the issue. If they do, continue to deflect: "Do you think the president has time for you?" "Yeah, right—like the White House is going to bother with your case," or "The president? I have no authority to go to the president. No one here does. You've been watching too much TV." Most lower-level terrorists will buy the first three arguments; the remaining will be dissuaded by some variation of the last three. If a person insists on a presidential pardon, you may need to proceed to step two, on the following page.

PRESIDENT DAVID PALMER

PRESIDENT JOHN KEELER

PRESIDENT CHARLES LOGAN

PRESIDENT WAYNE PALMER

2. CONSULT WITH YOUR SUPERIORS.

Brief your SAC or other superior with all information necessary to make this decision. Share all details
that explain why this candidate is worthy of presidential pardon. Such a decision is difficult, but typically a good pardon case will have some or all of the following attributes:

- The prisoner knows critical information that cannot be obtained any other way
- The prisoner is expected to cooperate fully once his or her demands have been met
- The prisoner specifically invoked the president's power to pardon and will not be dissuaded
- Time is of the essence

3. CONSULT WITH CTU FIELD AGENTS.

Before approaching the president, all SACs or superiors must consult with CTU field agents, who may
have developed late-breaking leads that may render the prisoner's cooperation unnecessary. If no leads
are forthcoming, make no promises to the prisoner and proceed to the next step.

4. CONTACT AND BRIEF THE PRESIDENT.

To ascertain whether to grant a pardon, the president will need as much information as possible. You will
be expected to summarize the prisoner's dossier, the up-to-the-minute situation in the field, and CTU's
assessment and recommendation. It is your responsibility to be sure all four of the criteria listed in step

195
194
193
192
191
190
189
188
187
186
185
184
183
182
181
180
179
178
177
176
175
174
173
172
171
170
169
168
167

2 above, have been met. Answer all questions thoroughly but succinctly and await the president's response. If the answer is no, that answer is final. If the answer is yes, the president's staff will take the next steps with the attorney general.

5. PROVIDE DELIVERY INSTRUCTIONS TO THE PRESIDENT'S STAFF.

Recently it has become common for well-funded terrorists to request that a signed document be faxed to attorneys located on foreign soil. Given time constraints proof of fax and production of the original document are usually sufficient to persuade them to uphold their end of the agreement. Whatever the arrangements for delivery, make no further promises or statements to the prisoner until the signed agreement—either an original or a fax—is in hand.

6. DEBRIEF THE PRISONER AND DETERMINE RELEASE PROTOCOL.

Remember, *pardon* is not a code word for *release*. The language of most immunity/pardon agreements usually stipulates that the prisoner's information proves to be relevant and accurate and that it results in the successful apprehension of hostiles. For this reason, CTU will not release a prisoner until the information supplied is verified, and the immediate threat has been eliminated. There may also be tactical value in "detaining" a prisoner. He or she may be needed in a prisoner exchange. He or she may still be wanted on charges in foreign countries, and it is your duty to follow up on this possibility. Upon conclusion of an operation, deportation and extradition are excellent alternatives to simply releasing the prisoner into the U.S. population.

IMPORTANT

You must be prepared for unusual pardon/immunity situations and act nimbly as the situation warrants. On Day 2, traitor Nina Myers sought pardon prior to committing a crime, namely the murder of Agent Bauer. Though this request was specious and manipulative, it was nevertheless honored by the late President David Palmer because Myers alone had information crucial to locating the handlers of a nuclear weapon. On Day 6, the White House agreed to give a pardon to former terrorist Hamri al-Assad before he requested it, an unusual break with protocol. The administration under President Wayne Palmer felt it needed al-Assad's cooperation so desperately that it could not wait for CTU to proceed through each of the above steps. The lesson: We are constantly rewriting the laws. Get used to it.

ON DAY 5, INFORMATION BROKER COLLETTE STENGER WAS GRANTED IMMUNITY IN EXCHANGE FOR NAMING ONE OF HER CONFIDENTIAL SOURCES.

195
185
194
193
192
191
190
189
188
187
186
185
184
183
182
181
180
179
178
177
176
175
174
173
172
171
170
169
168

G | DISASTER MANAGEMENT

AS HARD AS WE AT CTU STRIVE TO STOP DISASTER BEFORE IT STRIKES, WE ARE NOT ALWAYS SUCCESSFUL. BUT SUCCESS IS OFTEN A MATTER OF PERSPECTIVE. EVEN WHEN AN ATTACK HAS BEEN "SUCCESSFULLY" LAUNCHED, OUR HANDLING OF THAT ATTACK WILL BE THE ULTIMATE MEASURE OF OUR SUCCESS AS AN AGENCY. AT CTU WE PRIDE OURSELVES ON BEING PREPARED TO HANDLE ANY AND ALL SITUATIONS, NO MATTER HOW DIRE, AND WE HAVE TO ACCOMPLISH ALL OF THIS WHILE THE CLOCK IS TICKING.

199
198
197
196
195
194
193
192
191
190
189
188
187
186
185
184
183
182
181
180
179
178
177
176
175
174
173
172
171

Terrorists thrive on instilling fear, disrupting the flow of everyday life, and fostering doubt in the minds of citizens about their government's ability to protect them. These events—whether they're bio-attacks, dirty bombs, or other fear-inducing tactics—can affect small or large parts of the population. Many of these attacks do more to damage the psyche and morale of the people of this country than the health of the individuals themselves. That does not mean that they are any less of a threat to our homes, our health, and our way of life.

HOW TO HANDLE THE RELEASE OF BIOLOGICAL AND CHEMICAL WEAPONS

It is not enough to find, apprehend, prosecute, and imprison the terrorists responsible for attacks on U.S. soil. Their "success" in executing an attack is only a success if we allow it to be. Controlling these attacks and containing resulting panic will help take the *terror* out of *terrorism*.

Two of the most challenging days in CTU history—both of which have been detailed in this handbook—involved the release of chemical and biological weapons into the general populace. Quick thinking and decisive action on the part of our agents were the only reasons these despicable and cowardly attacks did not develop into full-scale epidemics that would have cost the lives of millions of citizens.

The Biological and Toxin Weapons Convention of 1972 forbids the creation, production, stockpiling, and purchase of biological weapons. Unfortunately, terrorists refuse to heed or respect internationally ratified treaties. Therefore we must be prepared to deal with the aftermath of just such threats.

Terrorists have targeted several diseases for possible weaponization, including cholera, bubonic plague, smallpox, and Rocky Mountain spotted fever.

Some biological weapons are infective, others are not. Anthrax, for example,

200
199
198
197
196
195
194
193
192
191
190
189
188
187
186
185
184
163
162
181
180
179
178
177
176
175
174
173
172

THE RELEASE OF NERVE GAS IN A
SHOPPING MALL ON DAY 5 LED TO A
SWIFT EVACUATION OF CIVILIANS.

201
200
199
198
197
196
195
194
193
192
191
190

often affects only the person exposed. The Cordilla virus, by contrast, is highly contagious once the host exceeds the virus's dormant period. Chemical weapons vary in shape and size. Military organizations worldwide have for many years developed various types of nerve gas. Although such gases are rarely contagious, they act much more quickly than biological weapons.

This section does not provide specifics of the weapons themselves (see additional information in section B3, "Understanding the Terrorist Arsenal," page 57).

It is about what *you*, as an agent of CTU, can do after the fact to minimize suffering, damage, and chaos—thus saving both precious lives and valuable time.

Always do your best to keep the following in mind.

189
188
187
186
185
184
183
182
181
180
179
178
177
176
175
174
173

FIRST AND FOREMOST, CONTAIN THOSE WHO HAVE BEEN INFECTED.

Remember that you may not initially know exactly what kind of biological or chemical agent has been used in an attack. Therefore you must quarantine those who may have been exposed until you can determine precisely what it is you're dealing with. Always err on the side of caution. Quick thinking by CTU agents at the Chandler Hotel in Los Angeles prevented the Cordilla virus from spreading throughout Los Angeles.

ALERT THE APPROPRIATE AGENCIES.

To find out what you're dealing with, you will have to enlist the help of agencies specializing in these types of weapons. Early communication with the Centers for Disease Control, Hazmat, the Chemical Response Team, and/or local law enforcement can help identify the kind of weapon used. Armed with pertinent information, you will be better able to treat those who have been exposed and to contain or eliminate additional outbreaks.

MAINTAIN CONTROL AND CALM.

Let the crowd know that you are in control. Instill a sense of calm by exuding that composure yourself. Making individuals act as you need without supplying all the information they want can be difficult. Sometimes the deception of a few can benefit the welfare of many. When guests at the Chandler Hotel inquired why they were not permitted to leave the hotel, they were informed that a dangerous virus had been released outside, not inside, the building. That was a lie, but it initially kept the vast majority of guests from exiting the hotel and infecting others.

202
201
200
199
198
197
196
195
194
193
192
191
190
189
188
187
186
185

Use force if necessary. You may be compelled to terminate, with extreme prejudice, any citizen who refuses to comply with your directives. Do what you must to protect the larger population. No one welcomes these situations, and executing such a task may cause emotional distress in some agents. Please seek CTU's counseling unit for assistance.

ON DAY 3, GUESTS AT THE CHANDLER HOTEL WERE INJURED AND KILLED BY THE CORDILLA VIRUS, A HIGHLY CONTAGIOUS BIOLOGICAL WEAPON.

To improve your techniques and extend your comfort level in this area, we highly recommend logging as many hours as possible in Disaster Control Simulation. This training program now has an additional certification program, which is available not only to CTU agents but also to qualified representatives from other federal agencies. This interagency certification program was created in honor of the late Michelle Dessler, whose handling of the Cordilla virus attack at the Chandler Hotel demonstrated exemplary skill and bravery and earned numerous commendations. See your supervisor for further information about registration and requirements.

180
179
178
177
176
175
174
173

DISASTER MANAGEMENT 61

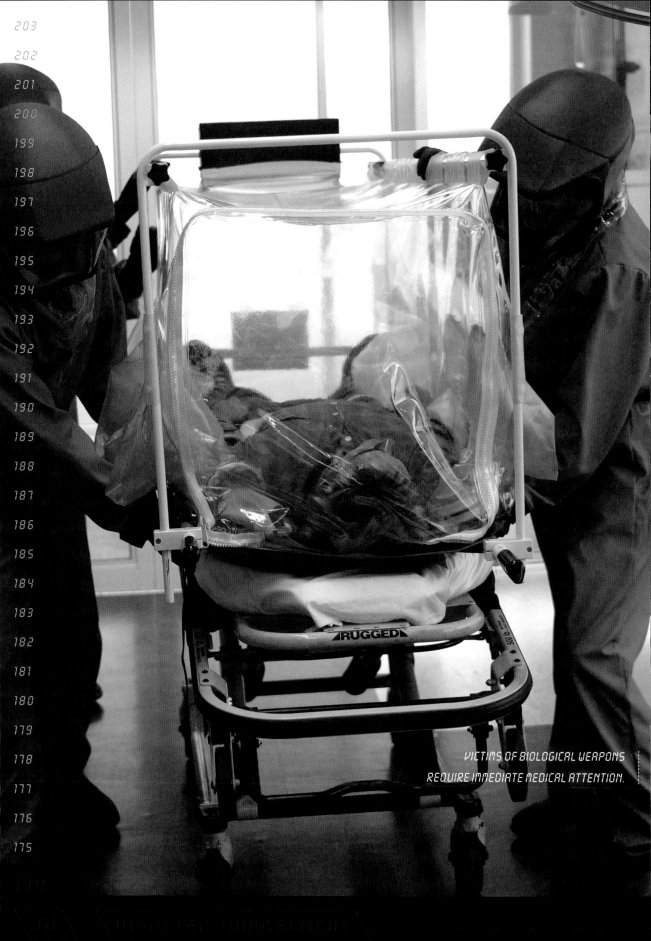

VICTIMS OF BIOLOGICAL WEAPONS
REQUIRE IMMEDIATE MEDICAL ATTENTION.

204
203
202
201
200
199
198
197
196
195
194
193
192
191
190
189
188
187
186
185
184
183
182
181
180
179
178
177
176

BE JUDICIOUS WITH INFORMATION.

Let agents from the CTU media-relations department do their jobs. Do not, under any circumstances, release any information related to a biological or chemical attack unless you are given specific permission or instruction to do so. Do not assume that it is permissable to release facts unless directed and, most important, do not make assumptions about what the facts are and to whom you may communicate them.

CONSIDER ALL TARGETS.

As you follow up leads and seek to identify additional potential targets for attacks, keep in mind that not all chemical and biological weapons are intended to target humans. Bioweapons, in particular, may be used to target crops, livestock, or water supplies as well.

TAKE ACTION IF YOU IDENTIFY A DISPERSAL DEVICE.

A variety of delivery options are available for the release of chemical and biological weapons. In CTU's considerable experience with these weapons, both Sentox nerve gas and the Cordilla virus were delivered via timed, programmable dispersal units. If you come in contact with such a dispersal device, move it immediately into the appropriate containment unit, if one is already on-site. Do so with extreme caution to avoid inadvertently detonating the device. Defuse the unit if time is available and a qualified technician is on hand. If you cannot defuse the device yourself, and there is not sufficient time to call in the appropriate response team, place the dispersal device in an air-tight unit. In a pinch, a refrigerator will do.

ACT QUICKLY DURING AN ATTACK.

One of the darkest days in CTU history was Day 5, when Sentox nerve gas was released at CTU's Los Angeles office. Those who survived did so thanks to luck and quick thinking. In the event of an attack by a biological or chemical weapon, proceed immediately to one of the safe zones. On the main floor, the safe zones are the situation room and medical unit; on the second floor, the safe zones are the CTU director's office and holding room 4. These rooms have bioseals and, if properly sealed, will protect those inside for a reasonable time. Areas must remain sealed pending the arrival of the Chemical Response Team (CRT). Do not attempt to leave until CRT has secured the area. If you cannot reach a room with a bioseal, you can attempt to seal the room you are in with plastic sheeting and duct tape. Historically, CTU has kept a supply of gas masks in the armory. As a result of the Day 5 attack, masks are now issued to all employees and should be kept at your workstation at all times.

SEEK IMMEDIATE MEDICAL ATTENTION.

Acquiring treatment as soon as possible makes all the difference between life and death. In the case of many nerve agents, for example, the administering of atropine can be helpful until full medical atten-

205
204
203
202
201
200
199
198
197
196
195
194
193
192
191
190
189
188
187
186
185
184
183
182
181
180
179
178
177

tion is available. CTU keeps a supply of atropine in medical storage. After exposure to chemical and/or biological agents, individuals should remove and bag contaminated clothing, including glasses, contact lenses, and jewelry. As you remove clothing, take extra care to avoid allowing the contaminated clothing to come in contact with eyes, nose, and mouth. Flush eyes and wash skin and hair with soap and water. Those exposed to biological weapons may be contagious and may need to be quarantined.

THE CHEMICAL RESPONSE TEAM WILL TRACK ALL AGENTS ENTERING AND EXITING A QUARANTINED AREA.

ALWAYS STAY FOCUSED.

In a biological or chemical attack that could affect a large number of innocent people, you must come to terms with the fact that not everyone can be saved. Difficult choices will have to be made to ensure the highest level of safety for the greatest number of people, and innocent lives may be sacrificed. Knowing that you have remained focused on your mission objective may seem like small consolation given these harsh facts, but it may be the only solace you will receive.

206
205
204
203
202
201
200
199
198
197
196
195
194
193
192
191
190
189
188
187
186
185
184
183
182
181
180
179
178

G2   RADIATION EXPOSURE PROTOCOL

We are all exposed to radiation every day. Exposure can come from sources as minimally harmful as a trip to the dentist for an X-ray, or it may come from a source as powerful and deadly as the detonation of a nuclear warhead. Unfortunately, in our line of work, exposure to high doses of radiation resulting from terrorist activity is always a possibility. Nuclear power has become more widespread, medical treatments generate increasing amounts of radioactive waste, and "dirty bombs" continue to be accessible and easily assembled weapons employed by a wide variety of terrorist organizations. As a result, radiation exposure and methods of containment have become important topics at CTU.

There are two primary types of radiation: penetrating, or ionizing, radiation; and nonpenetrating, or non-ionizing, radiation. As the names indicate, penetrating radiation can enter your body and severely damage your cells, whereas nonpenetrating radiation will not penetrate your skin (though it can burn you). Radioactive material can enter the body via direct exposure, ingestion, or inhalation. The main forms of radiation, from least to most damaging and penetrating, include alpha particles, beta particles, and gamma rays. Radiation doses are measured in units known as rems by a device called a dosimeter.

The consequences of radiation exposure can range from no effects to an increased risk of cancer to radiation sickness and death. Radiation sickness is generally chronic, which takes time to develop and may result from an accumulation of doses over time; or acute, which usually results from an exposure to a large amount of radiation in a short period. Radiation sickness may cause symptoms ranging from nausea, vomiting, and hair loss to nosebleeds and skin burns, or radiodermatitis. Depending on the level of the exposure, treatments are available from the CTU clinic or another medical facility.

Three factors that determine whether radiation sickness will develop and how serious it will be are:

1. The type of radioactive material, including particle size and concentration
2. The route the material took to enter the body
3. The length of exposure

On Day 2, CTU head George Mason was exposed to lethal levels of radiation, which indirectly cost him his life. Although the levels and type of radiation to which Mason was exposed proved to be deadly, the steps he took immediately following his exposure are standard and should be followed. If you are exposed to dangerous levels of radiation, acting quickly can be your only chance at survival.

- Once you have determined that you are in a hot zone, immediately summon the Hazmat team and quarantine the area.
- Close off the room where the radioactive material is located. It may be necessary to close off the entire facility. If it is possible to do so safely, shut off any ventilation devices that may spread the material to other locations within the building.
- The Hazmat team will initiate the decontamination procedure for all exposed persons and will coordinate with CTU to establish an appropriate perimeter.
- Collect all contaminated items—clothes, jewelry, glasses, contact lenses, shoes, cell phones, keys, underwear, everything—and place in sealed bags.
- Administer a high-pressure decontamination shower for all exposed individuals.

After following these procedures, Hazmat will conduct a field analysis and work the scene to determine the type of radiation, particle size, atmospheric saturation, and length of exposure so that the best possible course of action can be determined. All exposed persons will be thoroughly examined.

Once an individual has been exposed, the exposure cannot be undone. However, depending on the kind of radiation, a variety of appropriate drugs may offer relief from unpleasant symptoms, such as nausea and pain. Several approved drugs can help remove the radioactive substances from the body. These include Radiogardase, also known as Prussian blue; pentetate calcium trisodium (Ca-DTPA); and pentetate zinc trisodium (Zn-DTPA). The type of drug administered depends on the kind of radiation. Potassium iodide tablets, for example, treat exposure to radioactive iodine. All these drugs are available through the CTU clinic.

Agent Mason was exposed to, and inhaled, high levels of plutonium. Once plutonium finds its way into the bloodstream, the vast majority will end up in either the liver or the bones. In the case of a high or lethal exposure, a victim can have one week or as little as one day to live. As Mason experienced, even with lethal exposure levels, there is a latent period during which exposed individuals are largely asymptomatic. As his sickness progressed, symptoms became more acute, and eventually his mental functioning was impaired. Victims of this kind of exposure usually lapse into a coma before dying.

ON DAY 2, CTU DIRECTOR GEORGE MASON
WAS EXPOSED TO LETHAL LEVELS OF RADIATION
THAT INDIRECTLY COST HIM HIS LIFE.

208
207
206
205
204
203
202
201
200
199
198
197
196
195
194
193
192
191
190
189
188
187
186
185
184
183
182
181
180
179

209
208
207
206
205
204
203
202
201
200
199
198
197
196
195
194
193
192

THE LATE INTELLIGENCE ANALYST EDGAR
STILES HALTED THE MELTDOWN OF
SEVERAL NUCLEAR REACTORS ON DAY 4.

191
190
189
188
187
186
185
184
183
182
181
180

210
209
208
207
206
205
204
203
202
201
200
199
198
197
196
195
194
193
192
191
190
189
188
187
186
185
184
183
182

HOW TO STOP A NUCLEAR REACTOR MELTDOWN

In the event of a pending nuclear meltdown instigated by terrorist operatives, time is of the essence. The only time in CTU history that United States nuclear plants came under the control of terrorists was on Day 4, when a group under the guidance of Habib Marwan came into possession of a Dobson Override device, which had been developed by defense contractor McLennan-Forster. The override is a highly advanced combination of hardware and software that allows a person to take remote control of a nuclear reactor. Ideally, this device would be used to prevent a disaster, but in this unfortunate turn of events, it was used to start one, sending more than one hundred facilities across the country on their way to a meltdown.

There are limited things that can be done to avert a meltdown, but the following approach proved useful for late CTU intelligence analyst Edgar Stiles:

• Hack through the reactor's firewall.

If all the reactors have not been taken over by the override, try to intercede and acquire a piece of the code. With this information, you may then be able to gain access to the kernels, or cores of the computer-operating systems, of the power plants. Accessing the kernels is not something that CTU normally has the authorization to do. On the day in question, Defense Secretary James Heller authorized Stiles to do so. Normally, no one—with or without authorization—is permitted to manipulate the kernels while the plants are online.

Once you have gained access and gotten inside the kernel, exert extreme caution. You could unintentionally accelerate, rather than slow, the meltdown.

• While working to put a software lock on the Dobson Override code, be sure to stay away from the pre-compiled headers. Be aware that there is a chance of causing a load imbalance. If the kernels are disrupted, the result may be a core meltdown of some of the reactors.

• If shutdown codes have already been corrupted, and the reactors are immune to the kill sequence, it may be too late. The reactors may be firmly in the grip of the override. If you are successful, however, you can regain control of the reactors and eliminate any threat of meltdown or overload.

• As with any highly charged situation that may result in the deaths of millions of innocent people, be sure you know what you are doing. One mistake and you may cause a chain reaction resulting in nuclear holocaust. The quick thinking and agile fingers of Agent Stiles prevented all but one of the reactors from melting down. (Ironically, the meltdown of the one reactor that Stiles was unable to get back online resulted in the death of his mother.)

211
210
209
208
207
206
205
204
203
202
201
200
199
198
197
196
195
194
193
192
191
190
189
188
187
186
185
184
183

63 HOW TO DISPOSE OF A LIVE BOMB

All attempts are made to find bombs and deactivate them before they become armed. Obviously, that is not always possible. Our bomb squad members are well trained in explosive ordnance disposal (EOD) and work closely with experts from other branches of federal and local law enforcement to ensure that crises don't develop into full-scale disasters. What follows are general guidelines of what to expect in the field should you encounter an armed explosive device.

CONVENTIONAL BOMBS

CTU assures all agents that the vast majority of conventional bombs can be easily dismantled. In fact, many can be deactivated using a robotic device, remotely controlled by a highly trained EOD specialist. Once an activated bomb has been identified, the following procedure should be implemented:

- Alert the bomb squad. Seal off the area and establish a safe perimeter. (For more information on establishing perimeters, see page 114.)
- If time, circumstance, and physical premises permit, send a bomb robot to inspect the device. Confirm the type of bomb, whether it is armed, and, if so, how much time remains before detonation.
- Use the robot to deactivate the bomb. CTU's current technology employs a high-pressure jet of water—commonly referred to as the disruptor cannon—or freeze-delivering device to "disrupt" the bomb's circuitry. (CTU is also experimenting with the use of radiation and lasers to disrupt circuitry.)
- When robots cannot be used, an agent must enter the danger zone and apply a hands-on approach. If time permits, the explosive device will be transported to a remote area or, better yet, to the bomb squad facility, where it can be safely dismantled with minimal risk to the general population.
- Transport the bomb in the "tank," a specially designed reinforced canister or sphere that can withstand a conventional bomb blast.
- Be aware: The bomb may be equipped with an antihandling device, which will cause it to explode or accelerate the countdown if it is moved from its original location. In this case, mov-

212

211

210

209

208

207

206

205

204

203

202

201

200

199

198

197

196

195

194

193

192

191

190

189

188

187

186

185

184

ing the bomb is out of the question.

- If a robot cannot be used, and time, or the device itself, does not allow for safe removal from the current location, evacuate all personnel except EOD specialists.
- If it is impossible to stow, transport, jettison, or defuse the bomb in time, the bomb squad will establish a safety circle and layer the area with a suppression or ballistic "bomb blanket" to contain some of the blast and bomb fragments.
- Place as much distance as possible between the bomb and all personnel and civilians.
- If only limited distance can be placed between you and the bomb; there is no time to apply a bomb blanket; and the impending blast will likely affect you, other members of your team, or innocent bystanders, be sure that everyone follows the procedures noted in section E8, "Surviving in an Explosion" (see page 138).

NUCLEAR BOMBS

In the case of an armed nuclear weapon, your choices will be severely limited. Decisive action must be taken to minimize immediate and long-term harm to all living things. CTU and other agencies work with a Nuclear Emergency Support Team (NEST), a team of scientists and engineers who specialize in handling nuclear devices ranging from so-called dirty bombs (radioactive dispersal devices, or RDDs) to full-blown warheads.

CTU was twice confronted with the disposal of armed nuclear weapons. Time was severely limited in both cases. Since standard EOD procedures could not be followed, quick thinking was employed to avert a nuclear holocaust.

On Day 2, a nuclear device was planted at Norton Airfield in Los Angeles by the Second Wave terrorist organization, led by Syed Ali. Though the bomb was located before being loaded onto a plane to be detonated over Los Angeles, it had been activated. The following procedure was followed, and it serves as a good example of how to proceed once a nuclear device has been identified:

CALL IN THE EXPERTS.

On Day 2, NEST specialists were immediately called in, and the area was sealed off.

Determine the type of bomb and amount of time before detonation. If a tamper-proof mechanism is found and detonation is imminent—as was the case on Day 2—a means of disposal must be chosen.

ALERT THE PRESIDENT.

Even if CTU is the lead agency on an active protocol involving the disposal of a nuclear bomb, we do not have the authority to unilaterally decide how the situation will be handled. The final decision comes from the president.

THE DETONATION OF A NUCLEAR DEVICE IS THE SINGLE GREATEST THREAT IN THE TERRORIST ARSENAL.

Weigh your options. In this case, the choices were to detonate over either the Pacific Ocean or the Mojave Desert.

Once the president has endorsed an option, proceed decisively.

CHOOSE THE APPROPRIATE INDIVIDUAL(S) FOR DELIVERING THE ARMED NUCLEAR DEVICE TO THE FINAL DETONATION SITE.

Agent Bauer was willing to sacrifice his life to save millions. However, former CTU SAC George Mason, who was left with mere hours to live as a result of exposure to lethal radiation levels, took it upon himself to fly the fated plane into a crater in the Mojave Desert, where the bomb, and his life, were terminated. This final act of selfless patriotism has placed Agent Mason as a hero in the annals of CTU history.

214
213
212
211
210
209
208
207
206
205
204
203
202
201
200
199
198
197
196
195
194
193
192
191
190
189
188
187
186

IN MOTION ANY NECESSARY EVACUATION PROTOCOLS.
ember, fallout can travel for miles, depending on prevailing winds.

ABLISH FOLLOW-UP PROTOCOLS.
t appropriate environmental and health agencies to follow up on the detonation's effects
cal citizens, plant life, animals, water supply, and so on.

PORTANT

re another common weapon in the terrorist arsenal. On Day 4, a missile launched by
organization led by Habib Marwan was en route to Los Angeles. Because the war-
programmed to detonate not upon impact but only when it reached its target, it was
o shoot it out of the sky, resulting in falling debris rather than nuclear fallout.

NEGOTIATING A HOSTAGE SITUATION

Hostage negotiation is arguably the most delicate task you will ever undertake
as a CTU agent. Only the best of us will be selected to enroll in the Level III
course that certifies an official CTU hostage negotiator—and few among you
will pass. However, agency policy is to train all agents in the basics of negotiation because you never know when you might be called upon to serve as a
negotiator. Hostiles behave erratically. On a whim, some will insist on dealing
with a specific agent because of a real or perceived bond with that agent, a
grudge held against that agent, or some other irrational reason. When this
happens, you may be called to act even though you have not received full
training. Rest assured that a certified negotiator will be summoned to the
scene ASAP to monitor all communications and walk you through the steps.
Should circumstances delay the arrival of a trained professional, here's a
refresher, taken from our excellent Level I course.

215
214
213
212
211
210
209
208
207
206
205
204
203
202
201
200
199
198
197
196
195
194
193
192
191
190
189
188
187

ESTABLISH SECURITY AND GATHER INTEL.

If you are first on the scene, contain the hostage area by securing the perimeter (see page 114). Debrief local law enforcement or any witnesses. At this stage, intel is critical. Find out as much as possible regarding:

- **The hostage takers and their motives.** Are they mentally unbalanced? Are they fleeing arrest and using the hostages as human shields? Are they politically motivated? Are they terrorists with a larger purpose? Could this be a diversion designed to blind CTU and law enforcement to a larger plot?
- **The state of the hostages.** How many are they? What are their ages? How many are male? Female? How many are children? Are any hostages dead or wounded?
- **The circumstances.** What weapons are the hostiles using? What communication devices? Where are their lookout posts? Is any other dangerous technology—such as explosives or bioweapons—on the premises?

It is not expected that all information gathered at this stage will be thorough or accurate. The point is to start the process. Minutes from now, your fellow agents will be collecting this data so that you can concentrate on communicating with the hostile. Just be mindful that during the entire ordeal, even the tiniest scrap of intel could be revealed as crucial when analyzed by a CTU expert. Activate your mental radar and report to the floor all that you learn.

RECEIVE PERMISSION TO TAKE THE PHONE.

Consult with your SAC or supervisor at CTU before assuming the negotiator role. If you are the most experienced field agent on the scene, it may be advantageous to have you act as field agent rather than negotiator. Under no circumstances can you do both. For tactical reasons, a negotiator can never be the person in charge. (See "Important," page 189.)

BE OBJECTIVE.

When you take the phone, identify yourself by name. Remain calm, even upbeat. Let the person know that you want to resolve the situation peacefully. Ask for the hostage taker's demands. From the moment you take the phone until resolution, you must treat the hostage taker respectfully. Always consider the situation as serious, even if the hostile appears not to do so. Never laugh on the phone, even if he or she does so. Never say no directly. Never promise. If the hostage taker jokes and seems to be expecting a response, respond in a deadpan fashion: "That was a good one. Now, can we talk about what you need us to do for you?"

216
215
214
213
212
211
210
209
208
207
206
205
204
203
202
201
200
199
198
197

COMPETENT NEGOTIATION HAS PREVENTED MANY A
HOSTAGE SITUATION FROM ENDING IN DEATH.

KEEP THEM TALKING.

Stalling and delaying are the chief tools of the negotiator. The longer the stand-off lasts, the greater the chances that it will end successfully, without harm to the hostages, CTU agents, or law enforcement personnel. The easiest way to achieve a peaceful resolution is to bog down the hostage takers with mundane details. If they ask for a helicopter, ask them to detail how many seats they'll need, the amount of fuel, etc. Remind them to attend to the needs of the hostages by offering food and medical supplies. When they agree to these offers, ask them to spell out the details. How much food? What kind? Avoid sounding as though you are nagging. At all times you should sound earnest, as though you are doing your best to help them. This

217
216
215
214
213
212
211
210
209
208
207
206
205
204
203
202
201
200
199
198
197
196
195
194
193
192
191
190
189
188

EVEN THE FINEST CTU AGENTS—SUCH AS
THE LATE TONY ALMEIDA—HAVE FOUND
THEMSELVES IN HOSTAGE SITUATIONS.

218
217
216
215
214
213
212
211
210
209
208
207
206
205
204
203
202
201
200
199
198
197
196

detail work will tire most hostiles and make them wonder if their efforts are worth the fuss. They may even begin to doubt—or forget entirely—the point of their mission.

GATHER INFORMATION.

Before things go too far, state: "I need to know how many people you have in there." Get the hostiles to spell out the approximate ages, genders, and health of the hostages. Use whatever conversational situations arise to glean clues about the hostiles' past: hometowns, political affiliations, family, friends, etc. Never yield in your quest for information, but do not allow the hostage taker to think you are prying for details to use for nefarious purposes. Back on the floor, CTU analysts will be using the information you supply to pull together a psych profile on the hostile and filter it back to you. Work the profile.

BUILD BONDS.

Your emphasis on medical attention, food, and bathroom breaks for the hostages has a secondary purpose beyond their immediate comfort and aid. You are forcing the hostage taker to see the captives as human beings, not expendable objects he or she can murder on a whim. Likewise, through your unceasing objectivity you are coercing the hostage taker into seeing you as an ally.

EXTRACT PROMISES.

Early on in your negotiations, train the hostiles to see that this hostage-taking business is a two-way street. If you do something for them (send in food, arrange for media coverage, etc.), they must do something for you (release a wounded hostage). In all respects, your relationship with the hostiles must be built on a system of "tit for tat," an even exchange between equals, but with one crucial difference: They are not permitted to extract promises from you. Respond to their most unreasonable demands— such as releasing enemy combatants from Palmdale Military Prison—with neutral responses such as, "You know I, alone, can't authorize that. I need to run that by the folks on my end. I don't call the shots here. I'll have to see what we can do."

195
194
193
192
191
190

I M P O R T A N T

Be aware that although your service as negotiator is critical, you are also the Tac team's worst enemy. If you are privy to all Tac maneuvers or plans, you might inadvertently misspeak and betray critical information. It is for this reason—and to maintain the illusion that you are just a cog in the machine—that negotiators are never permitted to be in charge of the field operation. Regardless of the progress of your negotiations, at any time the Tac team may mount an assault

219
218
217
216
215
214
213

on the hostage area with the permission of the SAC, District, and—in the case of highly sensitive situations—the president. If that occurs, information regarding Tac's movements may be kept from you, and you may even be fed misinformation to throw the hostage takers off guard. It may seem like a stab in the back after hours of yeoman service, but it is for the safety of all involved. Trust us: You will get over it.

212
211
210
209
208
207
206
205
204
203

G5 IF YOU ARE TAKEN HOSTAGE

It's entirely possible that someday you may be taken hostage. Regardless of whether the attack is being undertaken with terrorist intent, we expect all captured CTU agents to "work" the situation as if it were. That is the only way you can use your superior training to gather intel, protect innocent life, and thwart the plans of the hostage takers. By all means, do all you can to bring the situation to a peaceful conclusion, but do so wisely. This section sets forth suggestions for achieving this aim.

202
201
200
199
198
197
196
195
194
193
192
191

ACT EARLY.

If you are a highly trained field agent, you may have the skill to disable or eliminate one or all of the hostage takers. If you are an intelligence agent, you may be able to use your unique skills to observe your surroundings, establish communications with the outside world, and send word to your rescuers. If you do anything, act at the start of the hostage takeover, when the situation is still chaotic and the premises have not yet been locked down. If you cannot disable the hostage taker or are outnumbered, consider escaping. (You are more valuable on the outside than the inside.) If you cannot leave the premises but can elude the attention of the assailants, hide in a location unobservable by the hostage takers. That will allow you to monitor their actions and report back to CTU.

BE DISCREET.

If you end up corralled with the other hostages, be mindful that calling attention to yourself through use of your CTU-honed skills may mark you for closer scrutiny, or even death, and further jeopardize your

220
219
218
217
216
215
214
213
212
211
210
209
208
207
206
205
204
203
202
201
200
199

DO NOT ATTEMPT TO ESCAPE WHEN HOSTAGE
TAKERS ARE ALERT AND IN CONTROL.
AWAIT A FAVORABLE OPPORTUNITY.

198
197
196
195
194
193
192

fellow hostages. If you are going to use your special training, do so out of sight. If possible, steal away from the hostage group or assault a hostage taker when you are alone. It does no good to attack an armed hostage taker while six of his brethren are keeping watch over you and fifteen fellow hostages. The others will cut you down and harm innocents as well. Be smart: Divide and conquer. On Day 5, Agent Bauer hid himself in an air duct during the attack on Ontario Airport. From this location he was able to ascertain the number and well-being of the hostages (three were ultimately killed in the attack), the number and position of the hostiles, and the extent of their weaponry and technology.

221
220
219
218
217
216
215
214
213
212
211
210
209
208
207
206

205
204
203
202
201
200
199
198
197
196
195
194
193

TREAT YOUR FELLOW HOSTAGES WITH COURTESY.

We would expect nothing less of you as an agent of the federal government. Do what you can to make the other hostages comfortable. Remain upbeat. Remind them that others are working hard to rescue them. This positive attitude has a tactical aim as well. People under duress tend to behave in a manner that works against their best interests. If one person behaves selfishly or tries to curry favor with the hostage takers to gain a perceived advantage, others may do the same. The result is anarchy. But if one person stays strong and confident, he or she can be the rock that others model themselves upon. You, the CTU agent, can be that rock. Avoid assuming too obvious a leadership role, however, lest you make yourself a target of your captors.

NEVER REVEAL YOUR ATTACHMENT TO OTHER HOSTAGES.

On Day 5, Agent Bauer's captors learned of his personal concern for one of the hostages—teenager Derek Huxley—and used the youth as leverage against Bauer. In a hostage situation, it's best not to single out any one person as an object of your concern. In some cases, we have watched hostiles spitefully terminate an individual just to convince another hostage to perform some action. Admittedly, however, concern is sometimes impossible to mask. A hostage who is clinging to a toddler, for example, cannot hide the object of concern.

CONDUCT PASSIVE SURVEILLANCE.

Always be thinking. Always be collecting intel. Which hostage seems to be the leader? Who is the weakest physically? Who seems least confident with his or her weapon? Are there any conflicts among the captors that you can exploit? Keep your mind sharp by mentally cataloging these details. You may have an opportunity to relay them to your associates at CTU or use what you know during a moment of diversion.

KNOW WHEN TO ESCAPE.

It is unwise to attempt escape when the hostage takers are alert and in full control. But should the situation deteriorate, you may risk less by breaking free than by staying. If, for example, an unstable hostage taker begins attacking his or her superiors or the other hostages, it may be safer to take your chances fleeing than to stick around. Watch for the pivotal moment when someone snaps.

USE THEIR TECHNOLOGY AGAINST THEM.

On Day 5, Agent Bauer noticed that all the hostage takers were wired with explosive devices that could be triggered by a handheld wireless transmitter. With help from the CTU floor, he was able to configure his phone to an operable frequency and detonate one of the devices, killing one hostile. A similar situation may or may not present itself in your experience. Use what you can, when you can. If you can steal a captor's cell phone and use it later to relay intel, you have made excellent use of available technology.

THINK CREATIVELY; YOU NEVER KNOW WHAT WILL WORK.

The late CTU administrative director Richard Walsh, while being held hostage as a "civilian," purposely wet his pants so that one of his captors would escort him to a bathroom. Once out of sight of the others, Walsh promptly crushed his captor's windpipe, gained control of his weapon, and quelled a disturbing hostage incident in Seattle. If you are trained and able, act when you can—but don't fail. If you are not convinced you can succeed, don't be a hero.

BE PREPARED TO WAIT IT OUT.

You've taken the courses; you know the drill. The only thing that ends most hostage situations is time. With every second that ticks by, the situation creeps closer to a peaceful resolution. When your rescuers finally appear, make no sudden movements, get down, and ensure your hands are free of weapons or objects resembling weapons. Verbally instruct other hostages to do the same. Identify yourself as a federal agent when appropriate.

222
221
220
219
218
217
216
215
214
213
212
211
210
209
208
207
206
205
204
203
202
201
200
199
198
197
196
195
194

225
224
223
222
221
220
219
218
217
216
215
214
213
212
211
210
209
208
207
206
205
204
203
202
201
200
199
198
197

INTERNATIONAL RADIOTELEPHONY SPELLING/NATO PHONETIC ALPHABET

Below is the most commonly used spelling alphabet worldwide. It replaced the Joint Army/Navy Phonetic Alphabet and should be second nature to any CTU agent. Keep this list as a handy reference:

A	Alfa	J	Juliet	S	Sierra
B	Bravo	K	Kilo	T	Tango
C	Charlie	L	Lima	U	Uniform
D	Delta	M	Mike	V	Victor
E	Echo	N	November	W	Whiskey
F	Foxtrot	O	Oscar	X	X-ray
G	Golf	P	Papa	Y	Yankee
H	Hotel	Q	Quebec	Z	Zulu
I	India	R	Romeo		

SELECT INTELLIGENCE AGENCIES WORLDWIDE

The following is a list of select intelligence agencies worldwide. Please be aware that many nations, including the United States, have more than one intelligence-gathering arm. This list is intended for information purposes only and should not be considered complete. If your mission takes you to a nation on or off the list, you will receive a dossier on that nation's intelligence agencies and any relevant contact information. You should also take it upon yourself to become familiar with any and all agencies operated by that nation. If you spot an error in these or other circulated lists, please bring it to the attention of CTU's publications director.

Argentina: Secretariat of State Intelligence, or Secretaría de Inteligencia de Estada (SIDE)
Australia: Australian Secret Intelligence Service (ASIS)
Austria: General Directorate for Public Security, or Generaldirektion für die Öffentliche Sicherheit
Belgium: State Security Service, or Sûreté de l'État (SE)
Brazil: Brazilian Intelligence Agency, or Agência Brasileira de Inteligência (ABIN)
Bulgaria: National Intelligence Service

226
225
224
223
222
221
220
219
218
217
216
215
214
213
212
211
210
209
208
207
206
205
204
203
202
201
200
199
198

Canada: Privy Council Office (PCO)

Chile: National Intelligence Agency, or Agencia Nacional de Inteligencia (ANI)

China: Ministry of State Security (MSS), or Guojia Anguan Bu (Guoanbu)

Colombia: Administrative Department of Security, or Departamento Administrativo de Seguridad (DAS)

Costa Rica: State Security Directorate, or Dirección de Seguridad del Estado

Croatia: National Security Office, or Ured za nacionalnu sigurnost

Cuba: America Department, or Departmento America (DA)

Czech Republic: Czech Security Information Service, or Bezpecnostni Informacni Sluzba (BIS)

Denmark: Danish Security Intelligence Service, or Politiets Efterretningstjeneste (PET)

Egypt: General Intelligence and Security Service, or Al-Mukhabarat al-'Ammah

Estonia: Security Police Board, or Kaitsepolitseiamet

Finland: Security Police, or Suojelupoliisi (SUPO)

France: National Defense General Secretariat, or Secrétariat général de la défense nationale (SGDN)

Germany: Federal Intelligence Service, or Bundesnachrichtendienst (BND)

Greece: National Intelligence Service

Hungary: National Security Office, or Nemzetbiztonsági Hivatal (NBH)

India: Joint Intelligence Committee (JIC), or Intelligence Bureau (IB)

Indonesia: State Intelligence Agency, or Badan Intelijen Negara (BIN)

Ireland: Óglaigh na h-Éireann, or G-2 Military Intelligence Branch and Army Ranger Wing

Israel: Institute for Intelligence and Special Tasks, or Mossad

Italy: Executive Committee for Intelligence and Security Services, or Comitato Esecutivo per i Servizi di Informazione e Sicurezza (CESIS)

Japan: Cabinet Research Office, or Naicho

Jordan: General Intelligence Department, or Dairat al Mukhabarat

Kenya: Kenyan National Security Intelligence Service (NSIS)

Luxembourg: National Intelligence Agency, or Service de Renseignements de l'Etat (SRDE)

Mexico: Center for Research on National Security, or Centro de Información de Seguridad Nacional (CISEN)

Morocco: Directorate of Territorial Surveillance, or Direction de la Surveillance du Territoire (DST)

Netherlands: General Intelligence and Security Service, or Algemene Inlichtingen-en Veiligheidsdienst (AIVD)

New Zealand: Security Intelligence Service (SIS)

Norway: Control Committee for the Intelligence and Security Services, or Kontrollutvalget for overvåkings-og sikkerhetstjenesten

Pakistan: Intelligence Bureau (IB)

Phillipines: National Intelligence Coordinating Agency

Poland: Foreign Intelligence Agency, or Agencja Wywiadu

Portugal: Intelligence System of the Republic of Portugal, or Sistema de Informações da República Portuguesa (SIRP)

Romania: Foreign Intelligence Service, or Serviciul de informatii externe (SIE)

Russia: Foreign Intelligence Service, or Sluzhba Vneshney Razvedki (SVR)

Serbia: Security Intelligence Agency, or Bezbednosno-Informativna Agencija (BIA)

Slovakia: Slovak Intelligence Service

Slovenia: Slovenian Intelligence and Security Agency

South Africa: National Intelligence Agency (NIA)

South Korea: National Security Council (NSC)

Spain: Delegate Commission of the Government for Matters of Intelligence, or Comisión Delegada del Gobierno Para Asuntos de Inteligencia

Sudan: 'Al Amn al-Khariji'

Sweden: Military Intelligence and Security Service, or Militära underrättelse och säkerhetstjänsten (MUST)

Switzerland: Strategic Intelligence Service, or Service de renseignement stratégique (SRS)

Syria: General Intelligence Directorate, or Idarat al-Amn al-'Amm

Taiwan: National Security Council (NSC)

Turkey: National Intelligence Organization, or Milli Istihbarat Teskilati (MIT)

Ukraine: Security Service of Ukraine, or Sluzhba Bespeky Ukrayiny (SBU)

United Kingdom: MI6 Secret Intelligence Service (SIS) and MI5 Security Service

---

GLOSSARY OF TERMS

ACTIVE ROSTER: List of CTU agents currently considered to be on active duty.

AG: The U.S. Attorney General

AIR FORCE ONE: The private airplane that transports POTUS.

AIR FORCE TWO: The private airplane that transports the Vice President of the United States.

ARMORER: CTU agent or agents charged with selecting, purchasing, and maintaining all CTU weaponry and outfitting all CTU firing ranges.

228
227
226
225
224
223
222
221
220
219
218
217
216
215
214
213
212
211
210
209
208
207
206
205
204
203
202
201
200

ARTIFACTS: Audio clues embedded in audio recordings that attest to their spurious nature.

ATROPINE: Drug used to treat victims of nerve gas.

AZIMUTH: The measured angle or trajectory of a bullet.

BACKSLASH PROTOCOL: A procedure by which one federal agency assumes control over another and instigates a computer reset process that emanates from the central network. Usually used after a major security breach or in the event of a transfer of authority.

BACKTRACE: Any analysis of media intel that works from the received message back to its origin.

BALACLAVA: A military-style ski mask.

BETA-BLOCKERS: The class of drugs used by CTU agents to restimulate the body in an "induced" death.

BIOMETRIC: A measurable physical or biological trait used for identification purposes.

BIOSEAL: A protective, plastic door covering used to safeguard CTU employees in a chemical or biological attack.

BIOTERRORISM: The use of weaponized organisms to attack citizens for the purpose of terrorism.

BIOWEAPON: The chief tool in a bioterrorist's arsenal.

BOLLARDS: Heavy retractable posts installed around civic buildings and public places to block entry of motor vehicles.

BXJ TECHNOLOGIES: A defense contractor headed by Philip Bauer with ties to known terrorist organizations.

C4: A stable, military-grade plastic explosive more powerful than TNT.

CALTRANS: California Transportation Authority

CDC: Centers for Disease Control

229
228
227
226
225
224
223
222
221
220
219
218
217
216
215
214
213
212
211
210
209
208
207
206
205
204
203
202
201

CELLULAR NODE CLONING: A method of mimicking a cell phone's frequency to establish a listen-in.

CHEMICAL WEAPON: A lab-derived compound designed to act as a destructive weapon when used against citizens.

CIA: Central Intelligence Agency

CODE 6: CTU evacuation code.

COM: Standard term referring to communication, communications, or any device used for communication.

COMSAT GRID: See *grid*.

COMSAT: A communications satellite.

CONTACT CODE: A special authorization number, usually comprised of four or more digits and letters, required by agents and others to verify their identity and establish contact with government agencies such as CTU, the White House, or the CIA.

CONTROL BOARD: A remote communications node—designed to be used by POTUS and his aides only—enclosed in the nuclear football and used to communicate the president's intentions to far-flung military locations.

CORDILLA VIRUS: The weaponized virus used by terrorist Stephen Saunders against the people of the United States on Day 3.

COVER: One's false identity, or the state of being undercover.

CRT: Chemical response team.

CTU-1: Call sign of a frequently used CTU helicopter.

CYANIDE: A fast-acting, toxic chemical frequently used in suicide capsules.

CYPRUS RECORDING: An audio recording, now known to be spurious, that almost inspired a U.S. retaliatory strike against three nations on Day 2.

230
229
228
227
226
225
224
223
222
221
220
219
218
217
216
215
214
213
212
211
210
209
208
207
206
205
204
203
202

DARPA: Defense Advanced Research Projects Agency. An agency within the Department of Defense charged with encouraging, funding, and overseeing research and technology beneficial to national security.

DEGREE-OF-FORCE PARAMETERS: Protocols governing how much force CTU agents and others may use in response to a perimeter breach.

DETONATOR FREQUENCY: The precise radio wavelength required to set off a wireless explosive device.

DOBSON OVERRIDE: An electronic device used to control mainframes of all national nuclear power plants from a single central location; works via internet.

DOD: Department of Defense. *Also written* DoD.

DOSIMETER: A tool used to gauge a person's exposure to radiation.

EMP: Electromagnetic pulse bomb, or "e-bomb," capable of destroying all electronic equipment in a several-block radius.

EOD: Explosive ordnance disposal.

EPINEPHRINE: A natural hormone, also called adrenaline, used to stimulate the heart and increase blood pressure.

ESN: Electronic serial number.

F-18: A U.S. military fighter plane.

FBI: Federal Bureau of Investigation.

FEMA: Federal Emergency Management Agency.

FIELD CALL: A judgment or decision about how to proceed on an active protocol, made by an agent in the field.

FLAK JACKET: A specially designed garment used to protect the wearer from shrapnel or fired bullets.

231
230
229
228
227
226
225
224
223
222
221
220
219
218
217
216
215
214
213
212
211
210
209
208
207
206
205
204
203

FLANK 2: Antiquated CTU duress code.

FULL TACTICAL KIT: A traveling arsenal enclosed in a suitcase, prepared by CTU armorer for field agents on the go. *Also* a weapons package.

GO DARK: Term used to refer to an agent who has ceased all communications with CTU and is presumed to be acting on his own and without authorization.

GPS: Global positioning satellite.

GRID: The area under surveillance by a satellite.

HAZMAT: Hazardous materials.

HOSTILE: Any person who is an enemy of the United States or who stands in the way of an authorized objective.

HOT ZONE: A cordoned-off area that is the subject of an attack.

HOURLIES: Flagged intelligence data coming from outside agencies and sources, analyzed every 60 minutes by CTU agents.

HS: Homeland Security.

HYOCINE PENTOTHAL: A neuroinflammatory used to extract information from uncooperative detainees.

INFRARED: A section of the electromagnetic spectrum that is invisible to the human eye but detectable by special optical devices.

INFRARED SWEEP: The action of using a satellite to scan thermal energy to detect life forms.

INTEL: Intelligence or critical information.

INTER-AGENCY PROTOCOLS: Established system of behaviors employed when working with another agency.

232
231
230
229
228
227
226
225
224
223
222
221
220
219
218
217
216
215
214
213
212
211
210
209
208
207
206
205
204

IRIS SCAN: Close analysis of the movements of a subject's eyes under interrogation to gauge whether that person is telling the truth.

ISOTOPES: Variants of known radioactive elements.

KERNEL: The core of a computer's operating system.

KEVLAR: The brand-name plastic material used in bulletproof vests and flak jackets.

KEY CARD: An encoded plastic card issued to CTU agents and used to gain access to CTU facilities, for identification, and to share and transport data.

KILL SEQUENCE: A piece of code designed to stop or interrupt a previously ordered software action.

KRAV MAGA: A hand-to-hand combat system, originally developed in Israel, taught to CTU agents.

LE: Law enforcement. *Also*, LLE local law enforcement.

LEAD TACTICAL: A field agent or analyst charged with responsibility for a particular day, hour, mission or protocol. *Also* primary tactical.

LIE DETECTOR: Any technology used to determine whether a subject is telling the truth, including polygraph, iris scan, etc. Excludes use of medical interrogation.

LINE OF SIGHT: Having a clear visual of an object or subject for the purposes of surveillance, communication, or connection.

LISTEN-IN: The act of electronically eavesdropping on another's conversation via mobile phone.

LOCKDOWN: A period of inactivity in the CTU floor, initiated by division or district, for the purposes of investigating a security breach.

MCCLENNAN-FORSTER: The defense contractor responsible for design and creation of the Dobson Override.

MI5: British intelligence agency responsible for internal security of that nation's interests.

233
232
231
230
229
228
227
226
225
224
223
222
221
220
219
218
217
216
215
214
213
212
211
210
209
208
207
206
205

MI6: British counter-intelligence agency responsible for external security of that nation's interests.

MICROTRANSMITTER: A minuscule device capable of sending complex data, such as audio conversations, over great distances.

MICTROTECH H.A.L.O.: An "automatic," i.e., push-button, tactical knife used by CTU agents and others. Purchase of these knives is usually restricted to LE agencies.

MIN: The unique, 10-digit mobile number that identifies a specific mobile phone on a carrier's network.

MOBILE PARABOLICS: A portable antenna used for covert eavesdropping and conversation taping.

NEST: Nuclear Emergency Support Team; a federal team of nuclear scientists and experts charged with defusing suspected nuclear bombs.

NIGHT GOGGLES: Visual apparatus worn by soldiers, agents, and others that exploit thermal imaging, image enhancement, or other technologies to permit wearers to see objects in darkness.

NSA: National Security Agency.

NUCLEAR FOOTBALL: A special briefcase, carried by POTUS, containing all current codes for the U.S. nuclear arsenal and a remote communication node.

NUCLEAR MELTDOWN: Extreme overheating of the core of a nuclear reactor, resulting in destruction of the facility and release of radiation.

OMICRON: A U.S. defense contractor that researched and manufactured the Sentox nerve gas used by terrorists on Day 5.

OPEN-CHANNEL MOBILE PHONE: An untraceable mobile phone technology.

OPERATION NIGHTFALL: A military operation in Kosovo led by Agent Bauer two years prior to the events of Day 1, which targeted the Drazen crime family. Aspects of this mission are still classified.

OPS: Military operations, whether overt or covert.

234
233
232
231
230
229
228
227
226
225
224
223
222
221
220
219
218
217
216
215
214
213
212
211
210
209
208
207
206

PARDON: Legally absolving a person forever of paying the penalty for a crime; can only be granted by POTUS.

PASSIVE SURVEILLANCE: Surveillance accomplished through indirect means; i.e., when a tracking device, audio recording device, etc., is not placed on the subject.

PASSIVE TRIANGULATION: Locating the geographical location of a subject or object using the relics of data previously emitted by that subject or object; for example, the tracking of a hostile's mobile phone even when that phone is off.

PDA: Personal digital assistant, specifically brand-name PDAs modified by CTU analysts and used by field agents to download and upload schematics, dossiers, etc.

PERIMETER: A geographic area enclosed and closely guarded by armed forces of CTU agents, U.S. military, and/or LLE.

PHOENIX SHIELD: Computer term for a program capable of destroying a computer's firewall and hard drive.

PLAIN-SIGHT SWAP: An abduction technique in which an agent substitutes for the person taken without evidence of an obvious kidnapping.

PLAYBOOK: A book containing current codes for the U.S. nuclear arsenal, contained in the nuclear football.

POSSE COMITATUS ACT: Federal law that prohibits the use of U.S. military for the purpose of law enforcement. The National Guard is exempt from this law, but the Guard must be summoned by the government of a state, not the federal government.

POTUS: President of the United States.

PREEMPTIVE PRIVILEGE: The power of a federal agency to assume control of a case in matters of national security, preempting efforts of LLE.

PRISONER TRANSFER DOCUMENT: An official document signed by all relevant parties authorizing the release of a prisoner from a federal or state penal institution.

PROTOCOL: A case or caseload, or the work procedure algorithm being employed to bring it to a successful conclusion; an active protocol.

RDD: Radiological dispersal device, or "dirty bomb."

RECEPTOR BEACON: The searching mechanism used by a satellite to gather and form images.

REM: Unit of measure for radiation exposure.

ROHYPNOL: A sedative, illegal in the U.S., sometimes used to drug hostiles or meddling LE friendlies.

RPG: Rocket-propelled grenade.

SAC: Special agent in charge.

SAFE HOUSE: A secure location—usually a residence—used to house innocent citizens, witnesses, or CTU family members for the purposes of protection and debriefing.

SAFE ROOMS: Work spaces at CTU Los Angeles that offer refuge and can be completely sealed off in a chemical or biological attack.

SCOTUS: Supreme Court of the United States.

SDT: Sensory disorientation technique.

SECOND WAVE: A terrorist organization headed by Syed Ali.

SECTION 1 SECURITY REBOOT: The action taken when CTU must relaunch security protocols under supervision because of suspected breach.

SECTION 1.12: The section of the CTU charter that refers to the removal of an SAC or other superior from duty due to incapacity.

SECTION 2.3 REDUNDANCY: A method by which an SAC or supervisor may view all actions taken by underlings via his or her computer. Refers to the section of the CTU charter that provides for this procedure.

SECTION 32: Protocols outlining how and when POTUS will be moved out of state in the event of an attack.

236
235
234
233
232
231
230
229
228
227
226
225
224
223
222
221
220
219
218
217
216
215
214
213
212
211
210
209
208

SELF-DELETING FILES: Computer records designed to quickly and automatically wipe themselves from a hard drive in the event of breach by unauthorized persons.

SELF-PROPAGATING WORM: A destructive computer program capable of initiating a server-wide shutdown.

SENTOX: A VX-class nerve gas that was stolen by terrorists and used to attack citizens on Day 5.

SHARPSHOOTER: A short-range shooter, usually a member of law enforcement trained to deal with targets in urban combat.

SNIPER: A long-range shooter, typically a member of the armed forces trained to conduct reconnaissance and, when necessary, to take out hostiles from a hidden location.

SOD: Secretary of Defense.

STAGING AREA: A mobile command post, usually the rear supply area of a CTU-equipped vehicle driven by the lead agent on a scene.

STUN GUN: A device that shocks hostiles with electric prongs.

SUBNET: A smaller part of a larger network, connected to the main server by a router or bridge.

SUICIDE CAPSULES: Pharmaceuticals containing a lethal toxin that are consumed by captured individuals to evade imprisonment, torture, or both.

SURVEILLANCE PACKAGE: A kit of tools necessary to perform low- or high-level surveillance, assembled for an agent by the CTU armorer and enclosed in a portable case.

SWAT: Special Weapons and Tactics.

SWITCHING NODE: An electronic device connected to a larger network that is capable of routing data, phone calls, and other information streams to similar remote devices, usually to hide the operator's true location.

TAC: Tactical unit or team, similar to SWAT teams in LLE agencies.

237
236
235
234
233
232
231
230
229
228
227
226
225
224
223
222
221
220
219
218
217
216
215
214
213
212
211
210
209

TACTICAL EAR: An electronic communication device that is worn in an agent's ear, allowing for hands-free or concealed communication with associates on the floor. Also referred to as one's *com*.

TASER: A nonlethal stunning device that shoots wired electrode darts that can incapacitate a hostile.

TRANQ: A tranquilizer or the weapon used to shoot tranquilizer darts.

TRANSACTIONAL IMMUNITY: A form of legal protection that exempts a person from being prosecuted for a particular offense or group of offenses. Usually offered by a prosecutor to a minor figure to gain his or her cooperation in ensaring a larger figure.

TRANSMITTER: An electronic device that sends complex data, such as voice audio, to a waiting receiver. Bugging devices tend to be transmitters.

TRANSPONDER: An electronic device that sends a single, simple coded signal, usually when activated by an electronic interrogator. Tracking devices tend to be transponders.

TWENTY-FIFTH AMENDMENT: The Constitutional Amendment referring to presidential disability and succession.

USE IMMUNITY: A form of legal protection that prevents a prosecutor from using a person's prior testimony against that same person in court.

VCI DISTRESS CODE: A newly developed pilot's code, indicating "hijack in progress, terrorists intend to use plane as weapon." Current protocol is to shoot down such flights.

WHITE ROOM: An interrogation room.

WSN: A wireless sensor network, as used in anti-sniper technology. Sensors worn by Tac team members capture and relay ballistic audio inputs back to a central computer, which calculates the location of a hostile "sniper."

X-CLASS MISSILE: A missile employing stealth technology.